'For We Are God's Helpers'

The Life of Monsignor Anthony Brouwers —
Visionary of the Lay Mission Movement

by
R. W. Dellinger

Designed and produced by OPM/Catholic Creative Services;
3305 W. Burbank Blvd.; Burbank, CA 91505, 818-567-2055,
http://catholic.opmdesign.com, karen@opmdesign.com.

Printed by BookMasters, Inc., of Mansfield, Ohio.

ISBN 0-9762948-0-X

Printed in the United States of America.

Table of Contents

Preface

Lay Mission-Helpers and Mission Doctors associations are the legacy of one man.

Monsignor Anthony Brouwers recognized the contribution that Catholic lay men and women could make in the missions, at a time when the role of the laity was yet to be expanded by the Second Vatican Council.

His vision of men and women offering their professional skills as a service to the world, and as an expression of their faith, is one that continues to have an impact around the world. We hear from bishops that these programs continue to fill a unique role, not only providing much needed skills, but witnesses who walk together and grow in faith on their journey. More than 700 have followed this call to serve in 35 countries around the world.

Those of us who have served are blessed as our experience in mission reverberates in our lives. Today we work to continue Monsignor Brouwers' legacy — helping others have this opportunity to serve by working with local bishops in Africa, Latin America, the Pacific and Asia so that lay people can continue to share their gifts, live their faith, change the world, and see how the world can change them.

Janice England
Executive Director
Lay Mission-Helpers Association
LMH – Sierra Leone 1989-1993

Elise Frederick
Executive Director
Mission Doctors Association
LMH – Thailand 1978-1981

Chapter One

African Epiphany

After presiding at the first Marian Congress in Nigeria — to commemorate the 100th anniversary of the dogma of the Immaculate Conception — Cardinal James Francis McIntyre returned to Los Angeles in mid-December 1954. Pope Pius XII's designated papal legate praised the "successful labor" of bishops, priests and sisters in improving the Third World nation's spiritual, social and economic health.

But one of the five priests who had accompanied Cardinal McIntyre, the archdiocesan director of the Society for the Propagation of the Faith, remained behind in Africa to visit local bishops and missionaries. Over the next three months, he traveled by plane, Land Rover, dugout and on foot from one mission outpost to another, traversing the huge underdeveloped continent. His journey took him through Nigeria and French Equatorial Africa, from Khartoum to Johannesburg, and across the Belgium Congo into Kenya's dangerous Mau Mau region, through the Sudan and even up the slopes of Kilimanjaro.

From firsthand accounts, Monsignor Anthony Brouwers received decidedly different reports —

Monsignor Anthony Brouwers discovered Africa's need for lay workers.

1

African Epiphany

stories that would radically change his view of the mission fields and the special individuals who toiled in them.

He met a missionary bishop personally delivering mail and supplies in a truck because there was no one else to do it. Later, a different bishop told him on a bush flight, "Don't send us money, send us people. And send us lots of Indians, no chiefs."

His heart went out to three sisters in French West Africa trying to care for more than 100 orphans.

He watched a young Dutch missionary, who was not a dentist but possessed an extractor, pulling teeth under a tree near his church. More than 50 patients waited in line. Another overworked priest remarked, "When I left home, they gave me a missionary's cross. For 15 years I have had to do more brick making, digging, roofing and cement work than teaching religion. They should have given me a hammer and trowel with the cross."

And he talked to an Irish nun with only self-taught medical knowledge, who not only delivered 600 babies a year but performed appendectomies, amputations and other emergency surgeries.

"Everywhere, bishops, priests and religious clamored for spiritual and material help. Being director of the Pontifical Mission Aid Societies of the Los Angeles Archdiocese, this begging came as no surprise," Monsignor Brouwers would recall in the April 1960 issue of the *African Ecclesiastical Review.*

"What I did not expect, however, was the constantly repeated plea for lay help. Everywhere I saw priests and religious trying their human best to be doctors, dentists, nurses, builders, mechanics, plumbers, electricians, pressmen, writers, typists and scores of other craftsmen. I saw missionaries bandaging infected and broken limbs. Others were deep into the hood of a Jeep or tractor. Not a few were editing and printing native newspapers.

"They were the first to admit that they had little taste for the hundred secular chores and jobs which fell to their lot," he pointed out. "They had come to the missions to teach, instruct, baptize, administer the sacraments — *to save souls* — and they found themselves overwhelmed with everything else besides, often to the detriment of their priestly and more supernatural calling and abilities."

The solution was obvious to the 41-year-old priest. Religious missionaries needed "helpers" — lay men and women with practical skills who could free them up to concentrate on spreading the *good news* of Jesus Christ. So when he finally did come home, there was a new fire burning in his belly.

"I returned to Los Angeles in early 1955 resolved to recruit, train and assign lay men and women for short terms as voluntary helpers to missionary bishops," he wrote. "Thus, quite naturally, there came into being our humble program to provide lay mission-helpers for Africa and elsewhere."

These words appear to be carefully chosen and purposely understated. For the pre-Vatican II Catholic Church of the '50s — where priests and religious held the high ground over ordinary churchgoers — there was nothing "natural" about the laity assuming any new ecclesiastical roles, never mind becoming lay missioners.

Missionaries, after all, were supposed to be models of holiness, a benevolent state believed to be reserved ordinarily for those wearing white collars or to-the-ground habits. Lay folks need not apply. Even popular American culture seemed to concur. *The Nun's Story* was a best-seller, and Bing Crosby, playing the gregarious Father O'Malley, was the movie prototype for a hip, yet saintly, priest.

Although the Maryknoll religious community had experimented with sending out a small number of people-in-the-pews to its far-flung missions, no U.S. diocese had officially dared initiate such a laity-based international outreach program. And any diocesan priest who had the audacity to propose such an innovative missionary effort would have been laughed out of most chancery offices — and possibly had his clerical career placed in limbo.

Rome-educated, L.A.-savvy Monsignor Anthony Brouwers, who had a deep devotion to St. Paul, the first missionary, must have been well aware that by championing the cause of lay men and women he was in for an arduous fight. What he probably did not realize was that struggle with national churchmen — including Bishop Fulton J. Sheen, arguably the most popular U.S. prelate of the 20th century — as well as local church authorities would last the rest of his cut-short life.

Anthony Brouwers was a studious and somewhat shy young man.

Chapter Two

A Vocation in Progress

Los Angeles was booming in 1912, the year of Anthony Brouwers' birth.

Filmmaker Mack Sennett came up with the idea of the bumbling Keystone Cops; presidential nominee Theodore Roosevelt addressed a large crowd at the Shrine Auditorium; and a man named Earle Anthony took a brave business gamble to open the first gasoline service station.

During the first ten years of the new century, the city's population had tripled to more than 300,000. Big Red Cars of the Pacific Electric Railway Company had replaced old slow-moving cable cars. By the end of the 20th century's first decade, there were more than 500 of the 50-foot-long, crimson-and-gold cars, which could reach the amazing speed of 50 miles per hour on 1,000 miles of track.

One popular destination was out beyond the city limits to Lincoln Heights, a new suburb just across the *Rio de Porciuncula* (Los Angeles River) with its pear orchards, rose gardens and post-Victorian homes. But for true urban adventurers there were even more exotic attractions. Billed as

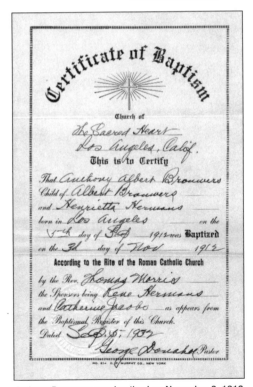

Anthony Brouwers was baptized on November 3, 1912.

A Vocation in Progress

"the one and only Los Angeles Ostrich Farm," the ranch bred, raised and sold the great birds to zoos around the world. The likes of Theda Bara, Gloria Swanson and the Gish sisters popularized the feathers in their stylist movie "vamp" gowns.

Nearby at a second farm on Mission Road, it got even wilder. One thousand alligators frolicked in 20 different pools. With its newly-hatched babies and up to 13-foot-long, primordial-looking reptiles, the Alligator Farm was a must see for Southern Californians.

The Selig Zoo, guarded by great stone elephants, was another attraction. The zoo, which housed lions, tigers, chimpanzees as well as real elephants, was the creation of film pioneer William Selig, who wanted an in-house African menagerie for his exotic jungle movies. Soon the only genuine zoo south of San Francisco became the largest private collection of wild animals on the planet. One of the early Tarzan movies, starring ex-Olympic swimmer Johnny Weismuller, was filmed there.

A decidedly tamer destination was Eastlake Park, with its swan-filled lakes, calliope and merry-go-round, plus beautiful botanical gardens. Visitors could go fishing, picnic, take a lovers' stroll or just listen to classical music from the bandstand north of the boathouse.

But the reason Albert and Henrietta Brouwers settled in what was then-called East Los Angeles probably had more to do with its multiethnic mix, cheap housing and job opportunities.

The Dutch immigrants would not stick out too much in a community composed of mostly Irish, German and newly arrived Italians. Albert found work at the Eastside Brewery, one of the area's major employers. (The others were the Southern Pacific Railroad, with its huge train yard and old car barn off of Main Street, and the City of Los Angeles.) And, like most of their neighbors on Hancock Street, the Brouwers family lived in a single-story clapboard bungalow with a small front yard.

Catherine was their first-born, followed on September 5, 1912, by Anthony and a couple years after by Peter. Young "Tony" and his siblings were raised in what *Lincoln Heights Bulletin-News* reporter Nelda Thompson described as a "Tom Sawyer life filled with adventure, truancy, early curfews, strict supervision and petty larceny — all part of the paradise of growing up in this new suburb with built-in grassroots."

Sister Mary Helen Bauer was born on September 22, 1912, 17 days after Tony Brouwers. She lived on Hancock Street, some seven houses away from

Anthony at around the age of four.

the Brouwers family. And both were in the same class at Sacred Heart Elementary School.

"I knew the family very well," says the retired religious, who served as Sacred Heart's principal for 17 years during the 1950s and '60s. "I would talk to his sister Catherine, and Mrs. Brouwers was a wonderful woman. Oh, gosh, she was great. A real mother who kept her children on track. They weren't running the streets at night or anything like that. She was a good neighbor and everybody liked her.

"The families then were all working class, but good, honest people. We didn't hear about divorces or couples getting married out of the Church. They didn't do that in those days. It's the way we were brought up. Just a close-knit Catholic community that still exists to this day.

"I never played with Tony in the street because boys didn't hang around where there were girls," she explains. "And he was kind of shy. When I would see him, he'd say, 'Hi! How are things going?' But I really didn't talk to him much, maybe just a little bit at school."

Diversity, Dominicans and the *Baltimore Catechism*

The world must have been a scary place in September 1918 for a six-year-old boy starting first grade.

A deadly influenza epidemic, which began in Europe, was sweeping across America from the East coast. By the time it ended a year later, half a million people would die. Czar Nicholas II and his family were executed, and a great civil war raged in Russia. Although the war to end all wars was winding down, there were 13.5 million casualties, including 126,000 Americans, when German representatives signed a November armistice in Paris to officially end World War I.

But the Dominican Sisters of Mission San Jose had already been working for almost three decades to establish a safe haven for Catholic children growing up in Lincoln Heights. Back in the fall of 1890, Mother Seraphina Maerz and two other Dominican nuns opened a two-room school for only 15 students. But the women religious, who traced their roots back to Dominic de Guzman (St. Dominic) in 12th century Spain, were not discouraged. And by the end of the school year, 58 boys and 57 girls in eight grades were receiving instruction.

When Tony Brouwers started school — with his parents paying $1.50 a month combined tuition for him and big-sister Catherine — there were more than 500 students registered at Sacred Heart. Many were the sons and daughters of immigrants from Ireland, Germany, Italy, France, Belgium, Austria and Mexico. Sodalities for all ages existed as well as separate boys' and girls' choirs who sang at Gregorian High Masses in Latin. The most popular sport was baseball, with junior high teams playing their games on the grounds of nearby County Hospital. The grammar school's big rival was St. Vibiana, the cathedral's team.

Students sat at heavy wood-and-wrought-iron desks with ink wells. Boys wore dress shirts and ties, knickers and suspenders, while girls dressed in plain uniforms with wide white collars.

Along with reading, arithmetic, geography and spelling, they studied German, Spanish, elocution, penmanship, orchestra, drama, art and music. But the subject that pervaded every classroom was religion — *Baltimore*

Catechism religion, to be specific.

In April 1885, Cardinal James Gibbons, archbishop of Baltimore, approved the famous catechism, making it the official religious instruction text for Catholic children in the United States. And the final abridged edition — *Baltimore Catechism No. 1* with its 208 questions in 33 chapters — remained the gold standard until the Second Vatican Council (1962-'65).

First-grader Tony Brouwers, like thousands of parochial school kids before and after him, would have had to memorize by rote the catechism's first lesson "On the End of Man," which was broken down into seven short questions and answers:

Q. Who made the world?
A. God made the world.

Q. Who is God?
A. God is the Creator of heaven and earth, and of all things.

Q. What is man?
A. Man is a creature composed of body and soul, and made to the image and likeness of God.

Q. Why did God make you?
A. God made me to know Him, to love Him and to serve Him in this world, and to be happy with Him forever in heaven.

Q. What must we do to save our souls?
A. To save our souls, we must worship God by faith, hope and charity; that is, we must believe in Him, hope in Him and love Him with all our heart.

Q. How shall we know the things which we are to believe?
A. We shall know the things which we are to believe from the Catholic Church, through which God speaks to us.

Q. Where shall we find the chief truths which the Church teaches?
A. We shall find the chief truths which the Church teaches in the Apostles' Creed.

A Vocation in Progress

With the soft-back catechism as his personal guide, he would also have learned about "God and His Perfections," "The Unity and Trinity of God," "The Angels and Our First Parents," "Sin and Its Kinds," "The Incarnation and Redemption," "Our Lord's Passion, Death, Resurrection and Ascension" and "The Holy Ghost and His Descent Upon the Apostles."

Later lessons from *Baltimore Catechism No. 2* would go into greater detail on the creed, the commandments as well as the sacraments and prayer. Tony and his classmates would learn about the difference between venial and mortal sin, the two great commandments and how to make a good confession.

Moreover, Tony would discover that the Catholic Church was "the congregation of all baptized persons united in the same true faith, the same sacrifice and the same sacraments, under the authority of the Sovereign Pontiff and the bishops in communion with him." And this one true Church was founded by Jesus Christ for a single purpose — *to bring all men to eternal salvation.*

Q & As 166, 167 and 168 could not have spelled it out more clearly.

To be saved, all were "obliged to belong to the Catholic Church" because "outside the Church there is no salvation." There was a loophole for other Christians if they had been baptized, believed their Church to be authentic and died free of mortal sin. But non-Christians, according to the *Baltimore Catechism,* were basically without hope. When Christ had his Second Coming to judge humankind, believers would receive the everlasting reward of heaven, while unbelievers would be cast into the fires of hell for all eternity.

As a result, every parochial school kid knew about the critical role missionaries played in God's cosmic plan. And every classroom, usually during Lent, collected coins for all those poor so-called "pagan babies." Because all Catholics — no matter how young — were obliged to save souls.

"When we were going to school, we gave to the pagan babies every Lent," reports Sister Mary Helen, the classmate of Tony Brouwers at Sacred Heart. "Little pink cardboard boxes, and every child got one. You'd put in money whenever you could. And then we turned those boxes in at the beginning of Holy Week.

"We also prayed for them," she recalls. "Because we knew these kids were the ones who would be put out in the street somewhere. Our money went to the sisters who ran orphanages, mostly from Asian countries. So this must have been how Tony became acquainted with the missions. And maybe that's why he worked so hard later on to help the missions out."

Sacred Heart Legacy

From 1937 to 1940, Hermine Lees attended Sacred Heart School, barely a decade after Tony Brouwers graduated from eighth grade. And even after 64 years, the Alhambra resident quickly recalls a teacher who turned her young life around.

"I came in the fourth grade from a Catholic school in Chicago, where the nuns did not think much of me," Lees says. "They told my mother point blank not to expect anything out of me. But I had Sister Mary Dominic at Sacred Heart, and every time I went to the next grade, she happened to be promoted also. So I had the same sister for four years.

"She was stern and strict, but in such a way that it was also encouraging and always flavored with gentleness and concern. She was able to really challenge every student. And she had a way of grading so that you always knew where you stood according to your test results. Because she would make it come out to decimal points — not just an A or a B in a subject.

"So because of her and this method of accountability, I went to the head of the class," she points out. "Me and a Mexican boy, Oscar, were always neck and neck. I felt encouraged, so I just worked harder. Without Sister Dominic's challenge, I don't know what my life would have been like."

The 77-year-old woman believes that a young Tony Brouwers would have likewise been encouraged to work hard at Sacred Heart School by the Dominican Sisters of Mission San Jose. Lees — who was a staff writer at *The Tidings,* the Los Angeles Archdiocese's weekly newspaper, and is currently the archdiocese's directory editor — also believes that a young boy could not have helped but been influenced by the tremendous ethnic diversity of the grammar school with its Irish, German, Italian and Mexican students.

And then there was the magnificent church itself at the corner of Sichel and Baldwin streets. The brick structure measured 120 by 56 feet, with a bell tower rising 130 feet. One of Los Angeles' oldest Catholic churches, Sacred Heart has loomed above all structures in Lincoln Heights since 1893.

"I loved the interior," Lees says. "I just thought it was wonderful. It was pseudo-Gothic, but not elaborately so. There were old statues and stained glass windows. The church had a sense of openness and sacredness. I know it made a big impression on me, along with the school, which changed my life."

The current principal of Sacred Heart says the urban parish school and church have altered the lives of children from generations of working class immigrant families in East L.A.

A Vocation in Progress

"We really get to know the students as much as possible," Sister Maria Elena Gutierrez explains. "And so, loving them in a guiding way and, hopefully, instilling in them the values that their parents are also working on and living out is our mission. Being Dominican, our whole thrust is study. Our motto, 'Veritas,' is very strong. We want the truth in our education to come through. So we strive to learn every single day.

"And every day throughout our studies, religious values come through in everything that we study," she stresses. "That has not changed at Sacred Heart in 114 years."

In 1990, when then-Archbishop Roger Mahony celebrated a centennial Mass of thanksgiving for Sacred Heart School, he praised the Dominican nuns for passing on those bedrock values and morals to thousands of young Angelenos. He also observed what a powerhouse of religious vocations the parish had been over the years — producing more than 30 priests and nuns.

After graduating from eighth grade, Tony Brouwers would soon be one of those alums who heard and heeded the sacred calling.

'Day-Hop' from Lincoln Heights

After a year at Cathedral High School, staffed by Christian Brothers, Tony Brouwers entered the new junior seminary, which was known as Los Angeles College, in the fall of 1927. The six-year program, made up of four years of high school and two years of college, was modeled after junior seminaries in Chicago and New York City. But there was one major difference: Los Angeles College was a regular day school, not a boarding school. So the teenager would take a Big Red Car, then transfer to another line to get from Lincoln Heights to Third and Detroit streets.

Los Angeles College had opened the year before with an enrollment of 68 boys. It was temporarily housed in an old convent until the new three-story brick building was finished that Christmas. Bishop John J. Cantwell celebrated Mass at the solemn blessing of the structure on March 27, 1927. Because the bishop had a bad cold, the president of the junior seminary, Vincentian Father Marshall Winne, read his speech.

"It should be the hope, the desire and the ambition of every Catholic family to so govern and spiritualize the home as to make it a nursery of children who, like the youthful Samuel of old, will cheerfully answer the call of God: 'Speak Lord, for thy servant heareth,'" Father Winne proclaimed.

The bishop's address acknowledged there were many people who believed that a junior seminary should be a boarding school, but stated: "I have confidence enough in the fathers and mothers who shall send their boys to this seminary to feel that, under their wise direction, and the cheerful cooperation with the Vincentian Fathers, that incipient vocations will be fostered and their children will continue to grow in wisdom and age and grace before God and man."

Tony's vocation did flourish at Los Angeles College in the midst of some horrific events.

During those years, which bridged the Roaring '20s and "brother-can-you-spare-a-dime" '30s, Hitler's Nazi Party rose to power in Germany and the stock market crashed. By 1932, with the Depression at its lowest point, more than 5,000 banks had closed and 12 million Americans were out of work.

Catholicism had become the nation's largest religious denomination by the turn of the century. And, according to writer Thomas C. Reeves, "many if not most Catholics were convinced that they were the future in America and already the superior guide in theology and morals." (*America's Bishop: The Life and Times of Fulton J. Sheen*, 2001, p. 33) But when Al Smith, the Catholic governor of New York, ran for president in 1928, he was defeated by Herbert Hoover partly because of his faith.

There is only anecdotal information on Tony Brouwers when he was attending Los Angeles College some 75 years ago — and not much of that. Probably the best comes from retired Bishop John Ward, who grew up in Los Angeles' Holy Cross parish but struck up a boyhood friendship with Tony while visiting his cousins in Lincoln Heights. The Brouwers family lived just two doors away.

"When my uncle died, my father kind of took guardianship of the family," Bishop Ward explains. "And every weekend we would go over there to bring them a barrel of oranges or apples. I had four cousins, so we'd be out there in the street with a bat and a ball on Sundays. As soon as we'd start playing, Tony would come out: 'Hey! What are you guys doing?' And before long, we'd have a game going on Hancock."

He said Tony was pretty much like any of the guys in the working-class neighborhood a couple blocks from Sacred Heart Church — except that he was older and a "day-hop" at the new across-town junior seminary.

"We had a real bat, a big ball like a softball and bases," the bishop recalls. "And we'd run to the bases right on the street because it was residential and not too busy. Whatever Tony did, he did well. So he was a good player. He could catch and hit a ball, but nothing demonstrative. No, he'd just get up there and hit it.

"But he always called me 'Jack,'" adds Bishop Ward, smiling and shaking his head. "Even as bishop, it was 'Hey, Jack!' He was really down to earth. A great kid."

Tony as a young seminarian.

'Interior Life' Thrives at Sulpician Seminary

The "day-hop" did so well academically at Los Angeles College that he was chosen to forego the normal California seminarian route and study philosophy for three years at the prestigious Sulpician Seminary back in Washington, D.C.

In 1791, the French Sulpicians had established the first American seminary at the invitation of Bishop John Carroll of Baltimore. The Seminary of St. Sulpice, which was later renamed St. Mary's Seminary, was also the first Catholic institution of higher education in the fledgling United States. The religious community — whose single-minded ministry was defined as "supporting, guiding, teaching priests and future priests" — would eventually establish six U. S. seminaries, including the one in the nation's capitol in 1917.

Tony Brouwers, one of the top students at Los Angeles College, had to be taken by the intellectual rigor of these men. Sulpicians in the 19th and 20th centuries were not only educators but the authors of scholarly books on Latin grammar, ancient and modern history, English literature, rubrics, dogmatic and moral theology, and scripture.

Their emphasis on instilling an apostolic spirit and zeal for evangelization in students also would impress 20-year-old Tony. And the Sulpicians had a special interest in the Society for the Propagation of the Faith, which the future Monsignor Brouwers would head 18 years later in the Archdiocese of Los Angeles. According to the 2nd edition of the *Catholic Encyclopedia*, it was "largely through their [Suplician] efforts, the Propagation of the Faith was established in this country and for a long time developed."

But it was his seminary teachers' abiding belief that a priest's own interior life — his heart and spirituality — was as vital as his knowledge and skills that struck an immediate chord. The evidence comes from a brown, 100-page composition notebook labeled "Quotations, Sayings, Maxims, etc." that the seminarian started on November 1, 1933, when he was 21 years old.

One of the first entries is from the poem "Quaker of the Olden Times" by John Greenleaf Whittier, which concludes, "And love and reverent fear to make our daily lives a prayer."

Later, carefully copied in neat longhand, is the story of a friar who asked his superior for permission to return to his cell during Matins (part of the monastic day's seven sacred holy hours):

"I am not," he said, "in a proper mood to recite the prayers."

"Brother," replied the superior, "for God's sake remain in your place. I assure you that if all of us who are not in the proper mood for praying should leave the chapel, there would be no Matins recited, and I should be the first to go."

And there are excerpts from a work entitled "Luke Delmege," including how a priest should adapt to the puzzle of life:

1. Dwell as much as you can with your own thought.
2. Make God your companion, not man.
3. Feed not on ephemeral literature, but on the marrow of giants.

The composition book also contains notes on preaching ("We must be very wary of figurative language in the pulpit when referring to dogma."), philosophy ("Philosophy is not taking things for granted."), immortality ("Surely belief in immortality is connected with belief in God."), ontology ("an inquiry into what is beyond man and the universe") as well as a host of other subjects. Plus, there are plenty of insightful literary odds and ends from the likes of Shakespeare, Longfellow, Boswell, Bacon, Paschal and Chesterton as well as Oliver Wendell Homes and Oscar Wilde.

And even an occasional little ditty, like "A Chaste Joke" on page 36:

"A young fellow went and told the priest that he and 13 others had been stranded on an island with a girl.

"Priest: 'Was the girl chaste?'

"Young fellow: 'Hell, yes, father. She was chased all over the island.'"

The most personal entry comes from a letter a proud immigrant father, Albert Brouwers, who spoke broken English, penned on December 18, 1933, to his well-educated son. By way of explanation, Tony writes, "Excerpt from one of daddy's letters, noteworthy for its genuine assurance for spiritual help. (slightly corrected)"

Then he copied into the brown notebook:

". . . but let me tell you, Son, from the bottom of my heart, you will be all right with the plans you got before you, and [I] pray that you will succeed in your studies and pray [to] God that you keep your health, now and forever in life. And Son, I your father will help you from now on in my prayers what little I do . . . "

During those Depression years of 1934-'35, Mao Tse-tung led the Red Army on a 6,000 mile march across China, Adolph Hitler gave himself the title Fuehrer, John Dillinger became public enemy number one in America and Shirley Temple sang "On the Good Ship Lollipop."

Tony Brouwers, meanwhile, was working on his master's thesis in philosophy at the Sulpician Seminary, which would become the Theological College of The Catholic University of America. His subject was Ralph Waldo Emerson, the 19th century New England transcendentalist; and his daunting scholarly goal was to trace the mental development of the philosophical essayist and poet from boyhood theism to adult pantheism.

Some of the writing in "Emerson's Idea of God" sparkles: "Ralph Waldo Emerson was born in historic Concord, 27 years after the Declaration of Independence, the second son of a Unitarian minister and a religious mother. His inheritance was seven generations of ministers, scholars, controversialists and fiery polemists."

But it is clear the seminarian's chief purpose is not to entertain readers, but to inform them — in a scholastic fashion — of Emerson's radical transformation. He proposes that four years of reading Platonic works at Harvard and the college's liberal environment made him an idealist. But Tony points out it was actually divinity school, ironically, that erased from the New Englander's mind "all adherence" to Unitarian dogma, replacing it with transcendental pantheism.

The second half of the 64-page thesis strongly refutes the doctrines Emerson came to cherish. In no-nonsense, almost harsh language, the future priest writes: "This theory [that man partakes of the divine Intellect] belittles human reason, making it but a passive entrance to the inflow of God. Such is manifestly an absurdity. If all share the same intelligence how is the diversity of ideas even on the same object explained? Surely Michelangelo and an illiterate serf did not share the same cognitive faculty."

The Master of Arts thesis concludes by lamenting the fact that Emerson's mental evolution was largely shaped by the times:

"His course was as radical as was the spirit of the age. America was not without its own Romantic movement, though sadly enough it far outstripped the liberalism and independence of thought, speech and art characteristic of the European Movement. Emerson is an exponent of his age's trend, and will ever grace the pages of American history of philosophy as the leading New England Transcendental Pantheist."

Life Lessons in the Eternal City

The final phase of Tony Brouwers' preparation for the priesthood began in the late summer of 1935, when he started his theological studies at the North American College in Rome.

Founded in 1859, the stone building at the base of historic Quirinale Hill, two blocks away from the famous Trevi Fountain, had been the training grounds for many noted American churchmen. Seminarians were handpicked by their American bishops — as was Tony by Bishop John J. Cantwell — to live at the "House on Humility Street" and attend classes at the Jesuit-run Gregorian University, one of Rome's highly regarded theological schools.

For the next four years, the 23-year-old seminarian would immerse himself in fundamental, dogmatic, spiritual, sacramental, biblical and moral theology. In addition, there were canon law, scripture, patristic and liturgy classes to master. He would dress like the other Americans, in distinctively cut cassocks trimmed in red, white and blue. And he would pray in the 350-year-old Casa Santa Maria chapel, which featured a copy of the famous *Madonna of Mercy* painting above the tabernacle.

A single theologian loomed above all others in the formation of seminarians in the 1930s — the Dominican friar and doctor of the church, Thomas Aquinas. Through repeated endorsement by popes, the 13th century saint's theology had taken on a quasi-official status in the Church.

Known to later generations as the "dumb ox," Aquinas went to great scholarly efforts to reconcile faith with reason. In *Summa Theologiae*, his major work, he examines the existence of God by using Aristotelian logic. God was the ultimate uncaused cause, and, as a result, the source of all order in the universe. Man was a rational social animal, who acquires knowledge primarily through sensory experience. And morality was derived from man's striving with himself, others and God.

Future Monsignor Brouwers and Cardinal Manning in Rome.

One might have seriously doubted the rationality of humans during the mid-to-late '30s — especially if one happened to be viewing the world from sunny Italy.

Civil war broke out in nearby Spain between leftist Loyalists and the forces of Francisco Franco. Americans, including author Ernest Hemingway, joined the Loyalists in their fight against fascism. Many priests and nuns were killed. And both sides conducted cruel persecutions and bloody atrocities.

The U.S. Congress passed the Neutrality Act, and British Prime Minister Neville Chamberlain made concession after concession to Germany and Italy through a policy of appeasement, while Hitler and Mussolini signed the Rome-Berlin axis.

The Japanese bombed Chinese cities and their troops seized Peking. The German army invaded Austria, then Bohemia and Moravia. Italian forces conquered Albania. Finally, in 1939, Germany used a new lightning war strategy called "blitzkrieg" to attack Poland without warning, starting World War II between the Allies and Axis powers.

Tony's early letters home to "Your Excellency" (Archbishop Cantwell) were breezy, concentrating on his busy life as a seminarian in the Eternal City: "Second year at the Gregorian is considered the most difficult of the four and so we owe a great prayer of thanksgiving to divine Providence who has seen us through another happy year in Rome. During these vacation months I am keeping busy with a little Italian and Spanish and various other subjects that are well nigh impossible of deserving attention during the scholastic term."

But in a March 39, 1936, letter, the seminarian made a bold pledge to his archbishop: "For the future, I can promise you my very best, spiritual, mental and physical, that the next few years may find me prepared, at least humanly speaking, for the inestimable greatness of the marks of Christ's eternal priesthood and the labors such a destination demands."

In an August 10, 1937, letter — at the beginning of his third year of theology — Tony wrote for permission to receive "Tonsura and Minor Orders" to the priesthood, employing a rather dramatic tone: "I beg of Your Excellency to send me the *call requisita* for ordination. I wish to receive these orders of my own free will and with the grace of God I hope to persevere in my holy vocation."

Fourteen months later, there was some really good news to send back home: "I am writing to inform you of my good fortune in receiving Priesthood earlier than customary." Later in the letter, he confided: "Naturally, as this information comes almost without warning, the proximity of such an important event spiritually and otherwise necessitates a certain amount of intense preparation. But the immediate goal, being what it is, makes the study even during the Villa [summer] season, a genuine joy."

And on December 8, 1938, the feast of the Immaculate Conception, 26-year-old Anthony Brouwers received the sacrament of Holy Orders in a solemn ceremony at the North American College. He had been a student for 11 years in three different seminaries. Now he was a priest in the line of the Canaanite priest-king Melchizedek, although he still had to complete the academic year and study for the five-day comprehensive Licentiate examination.

A Vocation in Progress

Newly ordained Father Brouwers gives a first blessing to sister Catherine on December 8, 1938.

In a letter to Archbishop Cantwell dated June 1, 1939 — seven months after being ordained early — signs of homesickness, along with the mounting horrors of the outside world, finally break into the student-priest's sheltered life of learning and prayer. But his words also carry a resounding sense of anticipation and exultation:

"As a delightful distraction amid the hours of study, I entertain the forethought of returning home. Especially is such a daydream pleasant when one can see himself arriving in the capacity of an eager neophyte in Christ's precious vineyard. After witnessing at close-hand the potential sorrows and wrongs in our world today, as the past year has so clearly demonstrated, one cannot but become influenced with an ardent desire to 'get to work' doing his small share to help effect a betterment."

Los Angeles flourished as a true metropolis during the 1930s.

Chapter Three

Coming Home to L.A.

While Tony Brouwers had been in Rome for four years studying to be a priest, a number of events had radically altered the United States, as well as his home state.

In 1939, Father Brouwers returned to Los Angeles.

The "Dust Bowl," the most destructive drought the Midwest ever encountered, turned the nation's Great Plains into an arid desert and Route 66 into a raging river of migration. Between 1935 and 1939, 350,000 so called "Okies" and "Arkies" packed their belongings and headed for the new promise land of Southern California.

Many wound up in the Central Valley as farm workers. The rest sought a second chance in Los Angeles. The city fought back frantically by dispatching some 130 cops to the California-Nevada border to turn away hitchhikers and "bums" riding the rails. In his "Talking Dust Bowl Blues," balladeer Woody Guthrie lamented that California was no Garden of Eden: "Believe it or not, you won't find it so hot, if you ain't got the do-re-mi."

In 1936, when Boulder Dam was completed on the Colorado River, Lake Mead, America's largest reservoir was created. Holding back 10 trillion gallons of water, the dam was the highest in the world. Los Angeles benefited with a surge of electrical power. And by 1935, at the start of recovery from the Great Depression, its populations swelled to 1,311,000.

The next year it rained 31 inches in five days, creating floods and landslides. More than 100 Angelenos died and thousands of homes were destroyed. Property damaged rose to $65 million.

Union Station opened for business on May 7, 1939. During its first three days of operation, a million and a-half people showed up at the Spanish Mission style passenger terminal, which soon became a city landmark.

By the end of the decade, Los Angeles County had become not only the nation's number one aircraft manufacturer, but also its movie-making capital. Some 90 studios spent $140 million making films in 1939. And the city's population climbed to 1,500,000.

What happened in the Church the year Father Brouwers returned home was summed up by a headline in the December 29, 1939, issue of *The Tidings:* "Catholic World Events For Year Intermingled Many Sorrows and Joys." Pope Pius XI had died and his successor and namesake, Pope Pius XII, was elected by the College of Cardinals. Like his predecessor, Pius XII pleaded in vain against the start of World War II.

Other church happenings included the end of the bloody Spanish Civil War and its religious persecutions, the cause for sainthood of Mother Elisabeth Ann Seton being proposed and the continual increase in the Catholic population, which now numbered more than 21 million in America. The rise had been steady since the turn of the century, when there were just 16 million Catholics in the country.

The Tidings' year-end roundup story also made special note of the "severe interference with the labors of Catholic missionaries by war and the elements, with the rich harvests of souls and bright prospects for the future in many mission lands."

Did the neophyte cleric, whose priestly life would be so closely tied to the mission fields, happen to take special note of these words? Maybe not. But they were hard to miss on the front page of the archdiocesan newspaper.

In any case, American Catholics were feeling their oats at the end of the 1930s, with 21,000-plus priests, more than 16,000 churches and 5,000 parochial schools dotting the land. And young Father Brouwers' spirits must have been buoyed as he waited in residence at his boyhood parish, Sacred Heart in Lincoln Heights, for his first assignment.

It would come via a brief, to-the-point letter dated September 12, 1939, from the chancellor: "His Excellency, the Most Rev. Archbishop, has directed me to write to you and ask you to act as Assistant to the Pastor of the Church of Christ the King in Los Angeles for the time being. You should report there as soon as possible."

A little over a year later, Father Brouwers received another letter from the chancery, the archdiocese's administration headquarters, transferring him to Mary Star of the Sea parish down by the ocean in San Pedro. He was asked to take up his duties of assistant pastor by October 25.

Parish work for a young priest was draining. As a rookie, he often received assignments the older priests, especially the all-powerful pastor, did not want.

His weekdays often started with the early Mass, which was celebrated at 5:30 or six a.m. After breakfast, there might be a funeral Mass to say and grave-side service to conduct. Then there were sick calls to hospitals, convalescent homes and even private residences. If he was lucky, he would get back to the rectory in time to grab a quick lunch before heading over to the parochial school to conduct a religion class or give a talk about chastity to junior high boys. After school, more likely than not, would find him directing some sodality group or coaching a CYO (Catholic Youth Organization) sports team. And the tasks really piled up after dinner, with instruction for converts, marriage preparation and counseling sessions, altar boy practice and young adult meetings.

During weekends, many of these same duties were repeated. Plus, on Saturday afternoon and evening, he would be in the "box" hearing confessions for five or six hours from long lines of penitents. And on Sunday, he might say two Masses in Latin and baptize half-a-dozen babies.

Even a new priest's nights were not free. As the youngest member of the rectory crew, he was expected to take most of the emergency sick calls, which came at all hours, and still be bright-eyed and cheerful the next morning in his pressed black cassock. It was no wonder that many 20-something priests turned gray before ever making pastor.

Early photos of Father Brouwers in Los Angeles show no gray hairs, just an inch-and-a-half-high, jet black pompadour that would make Clark Gable, Gary Cooper or any Hollywood leading man of the period envious.

Coming Home to L.A.

Father Brouwers, center, served as Bishop Manning's first secretary and master of ceremonies.

Marriage Tribunal Staffer and Bishop's Secretary

On February 24, 1941, the now 28-year-old priest received another major assignment. The official letter says he was elected as "Ecclesiastical Notary to the Service of the Matrimonial Court of the Archdiocese of Los Angeles. You will therefore be subject to call and assignment by the members of the Court."

Commonly called the "Marriage Tribunal," the body was made up mostly of diocesan priests with canon (Church) law degrees and experience. Their job was to determine if the broken marriages brought before them were canonically valid — in other words, whether or not they were true marriages to begin with in the eyes of God.

In order to answer this vexing question, many cases went to a full-blown canonical trial, where a "defender of the bond," who worked for the tribunal, defended the marriage during the Church's investigation, while an advocate, also employed by the tribunal, represented the petitioner (the spouse seeking the annulment). Testimonies from witnesses provided the body with information about the couple and their legal marriage.

There were two broad grounds for granting an annulment. Did both husband and wife freely accept and clearly understand they were making a lifelong commitment? And did both partners have the personal capacity to truly consent to form the marriage bond?

Today, the vast majority of U.S. cases coming before marriage tribunals are ruled invalid. (Some estimates are as high as 90%.) But in the 1940s, the percentage of nullified marriages was much smaller. Many Catholics, who sought to have their marriages annulled, were simply told by their pastors, "You're just going to have to live with it."

Father Brouwers brought to the Los Angeles Archdiocese's Marriage Tribunal a tremendous sense of compassion, according to Bishop John Ward. As a young priest himself, the now-retired prelate worked with his older pal from Lincoln Heights in the tribunal in the late '40s, and recalls how hard Tony labored over each file that came across his desk.

"He went into every marriage case with his whole heart," Bishop Ward reports. "He really tried to help these lay people get out of bad marriages. He did everything he could to get them out of invalid unions. Like with his mission work later on, Tony was real compassionate about helping people. And just like with the missions, he gave an outstanding effort at whatever he did. Just outstanding!

"I was the new kid at the tribunal," the bishop points out with a half-grin. "But you could count on him to get you over the bumps. If I ran into trouble, it was: *'Tony, what do I do?'*"

One of these stumbling blocks happened on Father Ward's very first day at the chancery. A gruff monsignor shoved a four-page Latin document from Rome into his hands, grumbling, "Here, go read this and you'll know how to handle the case."

In a semi-panic, the harried priest went down to Father Brouwers' office and pleaded for help.

"There were probably about eight fundamental forms, with 30 to 40 questions on each one, that you had to help couples and witnesses fill out," the bishop remembers. "And Tony had actually structured all the forms and the particular cases we were handling. He had this thing so mapped out that all I had to do was just pick out the right form and just follow it. He had done it all.

"I mean, he was great and very quick. You really had to know Latin in those days. I'd say, 'Hey, Tony, what does this mean?' And he would just explain everything in his plain-speaking way. He could put his finger on the problem no matter what it was."

Coming Home to L.A.

Bishop Ward has other fond memories of serving with Father Brouwers in the Marriage Tribunal. Almost every afternoon around three o'clock, the older priest would come to his office, slink down into a chair, light up a cigarette and say, "Well, Jack, what's new?" Then they would talk shop about the cases before them or just discuss the latest chancery gossip.

It was during these free-flowing conversations that the future bishop realized what a discerning and holy individual this older kid he had played ball with on Hancock Street really was.

"He kept coming back to something, which I didn't perceive at the time as necessarily a profound opinion," Bishop Ward says. "That a priest must always be ready, willing and able to serve as the *Church* wants him to serve — not as he thinks it should be done.

"It was only later that I saw how profound this really was. Because you've got priests today contradicting the Pope, contradicting their bishop. But Tony had it right: a priest must want to serve as the Church wants him to serve. And this was an idea he later tried to get across to priests in the missions. So it was an idea he kept his whole life."

After brief assignments as assistant pastor at two other urban parishes, Hollywood's Immaculate Heart and Mother of Sorrows in Los Angeles, the now 33-year-old clergyman was assigned as full-time secretary in the chancery. A year later, he became Bishop Timothy Manning's first secretary and master of ceremonies. In this position, he acted as driver, overseer and MC for whatever liturgical celebrations the bishop took part in — especially confirmations at churches across the sprawling Archdiocese of Los Angeles, which, at the time, also included Orange County.

"Tony was into everything in the chancery," Bishop Ward points out, smiling. "He'd chauffeur the bishop to the parish, and he'd get everything lined up. The first thing he would do was go inside the church and make sure the acolytes [altar boys] who were going to serve knew what they were supposed to do and kind of instruct them. For a confirmation, he was the one who did the final check. And if everything wasn't ready, he would help them get ready."

The bishop adds, "But all the pastors loved him because they didn't have to worry, even though it was their responsibility. Oh, he was really liked."

Chapter Four

Finding a Voice

Father Brouwers' notes outlining a sermon on grace.

As a seminarian in Washington, D.C., and at the North American College in Rome, the 20-something Anthony Brouwers attended preaching workshops and classes on homiletics. He would have even given mock sermons to fellow students and graded their public speaking abilities.

But all these academic exercises were just practice, a build up to when the cleric addressed real people in real pews or parish halls. There must have been some briefly uttered remarks after Father Brouwers celebrated his first Mass in the Eternal City. His first full-blown public address as a priest, however, probably did not occur until September 1939, when he was assigned to Christ the King parish in Los Angeles.

The entire talk is outlined in tiny letters on a single 3"-by-5" index card. The title — "Great to be Alive" — is peculiar with the address coming the same month World War II started.

Father Brouwers acknowledged the troubled times in his outline's introduction: "It's great to be alive. You and I have probably often had this thought. Indeed it is wonderful to be alive. But across the ocean the horrible spectacle of war wages with mangled bodies. And I am afraid thousands would not agree. They are cursed instead to many living deaths.

"However, purpose — not horrors or joy and material prosperity — is what life is all about. Our aim is to make ourselves and others realize the happiness of being spiritually alive through our Catholic Faith and Church."

The rest of the black-ink summary drove home five points:

1. Comparisons are odious, yet Catholics are entitled to be "glorious" in the gifts of faith they have been given;
2. Possession often lessens evaluation. As a result, Catholics often take their faith for granted. They should recall the words of St. Paul to the Ephesians: "We are a chosen generation, a kindly priesthood, a holy nation, a purchased people . . . who have been called out of darkness into God's marvelous light."
3. Catholics must consider the restless career of the truth-seeker. The Creator puts into their hearts a desire for Himself — a desire for perfection, justice and peace.
4. In the pagan world, people also have desire, but it's never satisfied.
5. Sincere searchers come to realize the journey to truth is long and wearisome.

The budding priest concluded with a quote from his beloved St. Paul: "'Give thanks always for the grace of God that is given you in Christ Jesus — that in all things you are made rich in Him, in all utterance and in all knowledge.'"

Prolific and Profound Orator

During the first dozen years of his priesthood, Father Anthony Brouwers made presentations to many groups on many subjects. He gave talks to altar societies and parish sodalities, women's guilds and Bible study groups, Knights of Columbus chapters and Sunday school classes, the Holy Name Society, Catholic Daughters and the Legion of Mary. He spoke to nurses and doctors, lawyers, businessmen, converts, young adults and youths. He addressed confirmation classes, parent/teacher associations and high school graduations.

In fact, by 1948 — the year he became director of the Society for the Propagation of the Faith — the 35-year-old priest had honed his public speaking skills to the point where he was appearing regularly on local radio stations.

A sampling of the topics of his talks reveals the breadth of his interests.

In an early address on "To All Men It is Appointed to Die," he stressed that death to the Christian was a release, rest and reward.

Speaking in September 1941 on "The Mystical Body in Holland"— his parents' homeland under siege by Germany — he summed up his hourlong talk with the dramatic lament: "Holland's Church has certainly received generously of God's blessing; one would think that much cooperation has accompanied the graces. So, here has been given a sketchy picture of the skeleton of the Dutch Church, that if the Nazi invaders pull down its structure, you will appreciate and bemoan the destruction the more for having known the splendor that was."

A year later, Father Brouwers gave a six-week class on the "enigma" of suffering. In his notes, he said Calvary was part of life and to earn salvation one must embrace the "true cross." He pointed out that there was no better teacher of this than the Blessed Virgin Mary.

In a talk on self-discipline, he stressed that mortification was not an end in itself but a "death to sin." Self-command involved three things: patience, prudence and, most importantly, divine grace.

Hope is what makes life interesting, and Christian hope — based on God's promises — transforms failure into success, he said in another speech. Revealing a nascent poetic bent, he urged members of the audience to "pray for an increase in hope, so when the storm lashes, the anchor will hold. And always ask Mary to help us get through the sea of life."

A lecture he gave in 1942 entitled "Spiritual Deafness" was significant for a couple reasons. It addressed directly the subject that must have been on most Americans' minds, with the United States declaring war on the Axis powers December 8, 1941, the day after Japan attacked Pearl Harbor.

The fighting was going badly for the Allies. The Japanese had taken the Philippines and many other Pacific Islands, along with all of Southeast Asia. German forces had reached Stalingrad and the Caucasus in Russia, while their U-boats were threatening to destroy vital Allied shipping.

Father Brouwers dared to ask if the war that had so quickly engulfed the globe was a "crusade or a curse?" A "token of love of God" or a "sign of godlessness?" "Proof that men were with or against God?"

In attempting an answer to these troubling theological queries of national pride, the priest made another departure from Catholic preaching norms of the day. He did not quote the Holy Father, or even some saint or bishop, but a devout non-Catholic — Abraham Lincoln:

"'The awful calamity of a war which now desolates our land may be but a punishment inflicted upon us for our presumptuous sins, to our needful reformation as a whole people. . . . We have forgotten the gracious hand that preserved us in peace and multiplied and enriched and strengthened us, and we have vainly imagined in the deceitfulness of our hearts, that all these blessings were produced by some superior virtue and wisdom of our own. Intoxicated with unbroken success, we have become too self-sufficient to feel the necessity of redeeming and preserving grace, too proud to pray to the God who made us.'"

Father Brouwers pointed out that although U. S. currency proclaimed "In God We Trust," Americans had become deaf to revelation and dumb in worship and praise. Popular culture showed the nation's true fruits through sexy novels and movies as well as newspapers and magazines pandering to the lowest tastes of mankind.

"Is it any wonder that our peace prayers are unheard?" the priest asked, rhetorically.

Again he quoted the 16th president of the United States, saying it behooved us to humble ourselves before the offended Power, to confess our national sins, and to ask for clemency and forgiveness.

"Pray for victory, yes," Father Brouwers stressed, in closing. "But first we must cure our deafness and dumbness, returning to family, honesty, truthfulness and purity. When the world returns to God on the cross, God will return to the world. Only then will there be lasting peace."

A River of Words

During the remainder of the decade, the energetic cleric would speak again and again on these topics as well as bearing others' burdens, love of God, the call to sanctity, anger, pride, marriage, motherhood, penance, a Catholic global strategy, the spirit of poverty, unbelief, death, authority, saintly sanity, heaven and the evil of loving money.

After he became archdiocesan director of the Propagation of the Faith, the priest started making audio tapes of some of his talks and sermons.

Father Brouwers had a pleasant, although at times, almost dry voice. His tone was in the middle-male range and remained there throughout 90-

minute talks. His words just flowed, with few pauses. The only indication he was coming up for a breath or changing gears, in fact, was a slight voice inflection usually followed by "Now, . . ."

His sentences tended to run a bit long, and phrases were often repeated — especially when he was making a point or summing up. But one usually led logically to the next, with the definite impression that all was moving forward toward greater truths. Moreover, there was an underlying conviction, which might be described as religious, in his speech that gradually grew throughout a talk. Yet, he rarely became emotional or sappy.

The overall delivery was semi-formal, with few asides or attempts at humor. Just a river of well-thought-out words, sentences and paragraphs. He sounded, in short, like a prepared and dedicated college professor who

Father Brouwers was a prolific public speaker, who made presentations to women's guilds, Knights of Columbus chapters, confirmation classes and many other groups. Here he delivers a radio address.

believed that nothing in the entire universe mattered more at this moment than what he was talking about.

Many examples of his dictional prowess are on display in a talk he gave to junior missionaries in March 1950. Entitled "The Body of Christ Which Is the Catholic Church," the four-and-a-half-page, double-spaced typed speech (a rarity for an orator who preferred just hand-written outlines) focuses on a favorite theme of the priest: the Mystical Body of Christ. *(Capitalized and underlined words appear that way in the original text.)*

"Each one of you has a body. You must feed it, clothe it and give it rest. You also have a soul which can never die. Your soul can do many wonderful things like thinking up answers to questions. It can also decide to do something or not to do something. Your soul is all through your body. It gives life to your body," Father Brouwers told the parochial school students.

"Your body has many parts. You have a head, arms, legs and all the rest of your body. Your whole body is made up of many very little things called cells. These cells are in your hands and feet and all through your body. Each cell has a special work to do in your body.

"This is YOU," he stressed. "You are a body and a soul who can never die."

And then he delivered his first zinger.

"Now listen to this. The Catholic Church is called a BODY. It too has a HEAD and many parts or members. It also has a SOUL."

It seems likely the priest might have been looking right into the students' eyes as he asked, "Are you surprised to hear this? You belong to this BODY which is the Catholic Church. When you were baptized you became a part of this Body. You became a tiny cell in this Body."

Then he asked, "Why do you suppose we call the Catholic Church a BODY?"

And pointed out, "Because St. Paul tells us that Our Lord meant It to be like a body. He says that the Church is like the Body of Christ. Of course, the Church is not the Body of Christ which was born of the Virgin Mary and died on the Cross. That Body is now in heaven. Neither is It the Sacred Body of Our Lord in Holy Communion. Therefore, to show this difference we call the Church the MYSTICAL BODY of Christ."

Followed by a metaphorical explanation:

"The HEAD of this Body is Christ Our Lord, and we are the members or parts of the Body. The SOUL of this Body is the Holy Spirit, the Third Person in God.

"St. Paul says that although we are many Catholics, we are all <u>one</u> <u>Body</u> in Christ. Christ Himself is the Head of this <u>one</u> <u>Body.</u> This is so because a body cannot live without its head. All the parts of a body belong to the head and are joined to it.

"So also as a Catholic you are joined to Christ through baptism. In this way you become a member of this BODY whose Head is Christ. The Head and all the members together are called the Mystical BODY of Christ.

"All of the millions of Catholics in the world are like tiny cells in this BODY called the Church.

"Our Lord commands that everybody on earth be a member or part of this BODY, His Church. Everybody everywhere — white, black, yellow people — must be members of this Body and be joined to the Head, Christ."

Father Brouwers told the children how Jesus Christ founded a church 1900 years ago by choosing 12 apostles, whose sacred job was to go forth and teach all peoples. He stressed that the Catholic Church, therefore, is not just any religion. It is the one true Church on earth, and Our Lord wants everybody to belong to His Church.

Next he delivered a second zinger, pointing out that only one out of every six people on the planet belonged to Christ's body, the Catholic Church, and how it was the goal of the missions to teach and baptize these people. But missionaries were needed not only in Africa and South America to convert the unbaptized. There were plenty of non-Catholics right here in the United States, too — including more than 14 million black Americans.

The priest said, "We owe these good people a very special debt because our ancestors kidnapped and enslaved them." Even after they were emancipated by the Civil War, blacks continued to be treated unjustly and cruelly, he pointed out, and were not allowed to enjoy the same rights and privileges as other American citizens.

"Worst of all, the Negroes were not taught about Our Lord," he stressed. "As a result, many millions of them today have no religion at all. We Catholics of America have not done so much for them as we should. We failed to teach the Negroes about the True Church, the Body of Christ, Our Lord.

"Therefore, today we must try harder than ever to help them to know Jesus Christ and His Church. We must remember that Our Lord said very seriously: 'By this will all men know that you are My disciples, if you have love for one another.'

"If we do not love and help the Negro people as our neighbors and brothers, we are not good Catholics," Father Brouwers warned, at a time when southern schools were strictly segregated, only a handful of athletes like Jackie Robinson were playing on major league sports teams and the phrase *Nigger Lover* was a common derogatory expression. "We do not love God if we do not love the people He created and died for on the Cross. We do not love God's children if we do not do all we can to save their souls."

Finally, with some urgency in his voice, the director of the Propagation of the Faith asked the junior missionaries to "pray every day and make sacrifices to help the Negroes of America to become members of Christ's living body, the Catholic Church."

Chapter Five
Missions Find Father Brouwers

By May 1948, Father Brouwers had his hands full with multiple assignments.

Another letter from the chancery, another assignment for Father Anthony Brouwers. But this appointment came from the very desk of then-Archbishop James Francis McIntyre, who was transferred from New York, where he was Cardinal Francis Spellman's chief administrator, to Los Angeles in February of 1948, a prosperous period in Southern California. Nearly 300,000 people would move to L.A. that year.

The prelate had been a $3-a-week errand boy on Wall Street who, after attending New York City College and Columbia University, rose rapidly in the world of finance. When he promptly retired at 29 from H. L. Horton and Company, an investment house on the New York Stock Exchange, he was offered a full partnership in another firm.

But the still-young McIntyre turned that lucrative proposition down to enter the seminary. In 1921, at the age of 35, he was ordained in St. Patrick's Cathedral and began another rapid climb as vice chancellor, chancellor and vicar general of the Archdiocese of New York while being elevated to auxiliary bishop, bishop and, finally, archbishop.

Missions Find Father Brouwers

In Los Angeles, the archbishop did not waste any time reorganizing the curia, erecting a new chancery and refurbishing St. Vibiana's Cathedral. He also established new secretariats and commissions for vocations, communications, archives, cemeteries and liturgy. But arguably his greatest contribution was to Catholic education. During his first 15 years in California, parochial schools more than doubled from 141 to 347 — at the astounding rate of 13 new Catholic schools every year.

Archbishop McIntyre, often described as having an iron will to go along with plenty of Irish charm, had Bishop Timothy Manning, a close friend of Father Brouwers, pen the official letter of promotion.

"With a great deal of pleasure I wish to convey to you the decision of the Most Reverend Archbishop, by which he appoints you as Director of the Society for the Propagation of the Faith, to succeed Father William J. Duggan. This appointment is effective on Thursday, May 13th."

The Propagation of the Faith had sprung from humble beginnings — specifically, a French lay woman and a family card game. The revolution of 1789 had practically destroyed the once-formidable French missionary effort in the New World. With three of the leading missionary societies gone, both vocations and monetary support suffered greatly. In fact, France only managed to send out seven missionaries between 1793 and 1798.

Nineteen-year-old Pauline Jaricot of Lyons was well aware of the Church's outreach problem. Her brother, a seminarian in Paris, wrote home often about the deplorable plight of the few French missionaries stationed in the Far East. Lacking the basic essentials themselves, these men and women were hard pressed to provide education, medicine and — most of all — hope to those they served.

One evening, watching a family card game, she realized how easy it would be to organize similar gatherings of friends and relatives to support the missions. Later, at a meeting in 1822, she and nine other women agreed to each donate a penny a week of their factory wages to the pious cause, adopting the name of the "Society for the Propagation of the Faith." Their first goal was to raise money for Bishop Louis Dubourg's struggling mission outposts in Louisiana. In three years, branches of the grassroots, antipoverty, evangelization society had spread to Belgium, Germany and Switzerland.

During the early 19th century, however, the fledgling mission fields in America continued to receive the bulk of the society's allocations. So much so that in 1829 the grateful First Provincial Council of Baltimore ordered: "The bishops and clergy of the United States make it a duty never to offer the Sacrifice on our altars without thinking of the venerable Association of the Propagation of the Faith."

In 1896, when an American branch of the society was incorporated, the first national director was appointed. A quarter century later, Pope Pius XI raised the now-world-wide organization to a pontifical society with head-quarters in Rome. Each country had a national director, named by the Vatican and directly responsible to the pope. Local bishops appointed diocesan directors, who would assist the national director.

As the society's director in the Archdiocese of Los Angeles, Father Anthony Brouwers now had three broad responsibilities: to foster a spirit of universal mission, to inform Catholics of the life and needs of missionaries, and to encourage prayer plus financial support for missionaries and mission churches. At the time, however, raising money was the most critical part of the job. Most of the dollars that flowed to Rome every year to support the Church's worldwide missionary effort came from one collection on World Mission Sunday — and the bulk of that annual collection was made up of American checks and dollars.

A Good Appointment, but . . .

It was a good appointment, according to Bishop John Ward, but not a very prominent one. He says his boyhood baseball buddy just "slid" into the job without any fanfare or celebration. But for almost the next 16 years — until the end of his 51-year life — the priest from Lincoln Heights quietly built up the local Propagation of the Faith office until it would sponsor the oldest lay mission organization in the United States.

"Now see, this points up what is fundamental for Tony," the bishop stresses. "Whenever he went into anything, he went in with both feet."

One of the first things Father Brouwers did was start writing a weekly column called "Mission Chats" in *The Tidings*. His initial effort ran 565 words on page 32 in the September 24, 1948, issue.

There is an almost lyrical quality to the writing, with a noticeable different tone from the no-frills, inverted pyramid style of the news stories.

"Across the piazza of St. Peter's and out beyond the sprawling whiteness of Rome, the Holy Father, the first Missionary in Christendom, looks over the world," the 35-year-old priest wrote.

"In his mind's eye, he sees other continents — in dank jungles, on torrid deserts and icy fields, Catholic men and women, toiling against every barrier of nature and the human mind."

Then the rookie columnist painted a word picture that would have made Faulkner proud.

"Deep in New Guinea, far up the muddy rivers of India, under the shadows of Chinese pagodas and on the coral beaches of the Pacific, he envisions missionaries, men and women suffering, aching and tired, yet intrepidly hunting down human souls.

"These heroes and heroines of God's Kingdom, everywhere, with strange sounds on their tongues and Divine charity burning in their hearts, spend and are spent in order to bring Jesus' saving name to some of the two billions who know Him not."

Father Brouwers pointed out that the pope's missionary zeal is concretely backed up by the Pontifical Society for the Propagation of the Faith, with its local branches in every diocese who support "the reapers" in God's fields. And in capital bold letters, Father Brouwers underscored a point he would repeat often in the future.

"**EVERY CATHOLIC BY BAPTISM** is a missionary, pledged before God to exercise this high calling by daily prayer and sacrifice and material help," he stated. "You, the lay apostles of Christ's mystical priesthood, must sustain His Vicar's human hands, to the end that as many as possible the world over may know the faith, the hope and supernatural charity of Our Lord Jesus Christ.

"Today, except the Catholics of America, there is no nation that is able to help materially and by religious vocations, the conversion of peoples without Christ across the sea. America has become in this strange decade the spiritual and financial arsenal of the Church, called by Divine favor, to spend every effort in quenching God's thirst for immortal souls."

The priest explained that many ordinary Catholics feel this noble zeal to save souls to the extent that they project themselves into the lives of distant missionaries. Prayer, good works and contributions, he noted, are the "magic carpet" to these faraway lands.

"To render the Catholics of this Archdiocese ever more conscious of a Divine call to such an apostolate, this weekly chat on the Missions is inaugurated," the writer concluded, "with the prayerful hope that its reading will inflame hearts with Christ-like sacrifice and generosity; and that His plea 'that they too may be one in Us, as Thou, Father, art in Me' may not have been in vain."

Father Brouwers' weekly chats would do that and much more. For the next 15 ½ years, he told *Tidings* readers about the trials and triumphs of priests, brothers and sisters around the globe who were bringing the Gospel of Jesus Christ to nonbelievers. After he founded the Lay Mission-Helpers and Mission Doctors in 1955 and '59, he wrote passionately about these unselfish lay men and women who devoted years — and sometimes decades — of their lives to serving the poor and sick in the Third World.

'My Brother's Keeper'

The week that the priest died in January 1964, *The Tidings* reprinted his entire column (entitled 'My Brother's Keeper') from its October 16, 1959, issue. An introductory note by editor Al Antczak said the piece "inadvertently epitomized the apostolic spirit which characterized his whole life."

The piece started with Cain's contemptuous retort to God in a field after he had murdered his brother Abel: "Am I my brother's keeper?" The columnist pointed out that this egotistical attitude strikes at the core of fraternal charity, and signals a point of departure from the ways of an all-loving God.

"This is no rhetorical question," Monsignor Brouwers wrote. "To be Christian, to be Christ-like, each of us has but one declarative statement: 'I, we and all of us everywhere are our brothers' keepers."

He observed that it is only by accident of birth whether we are born enslaved or free, well-off or impoverished, educated or illiterate, black or white, pagan or believer. He noted that the purpose of God's church is not only to baptize the world but to improve life on earth for those who are born into misfortune.

"I am my brother's keeper," he declared. "I am the Church, for with the Holy Father, with the hierarchy and clergy, religious and all baptized Catholics, I am a member of the Body of Christ which is the Church."

Then he drew a rather revolutionary conclusion:

"I am united to Christ, being a member of His Body. I am therefore related more closely than to my earthly parents and family, to all other members of this Mystical Body. I owe all my life and strength and means to support the vitality and continued well-being of this Body."

He proclaimed that as instruments of God, all Catholics, in short, are apostles of Christ.

"I too am on a mission, by virtue of baptism and my becoming a living cell in Christ's Body which is the Church, and by confirmation which provides me all the ability, energy and knowledge to perform my apostolic functions," he continued.

"I am my brother's keeper. I am responsible for his salvation to an astounding degree. God in heaven looks to me, not primarily to His angels, to effect the total conversion of the human race to His way, truth and life.

"This is the message of the missions," he stressed, "which can only be acknowledged and executed by endless praying, by constant sacrifices of the spiritual order, and by alms and material gifts calculated to fulfill the will of God, the salvation of each and every soul."

Monsignor Brouwers ended his signature column with a question, then a plea colored by the ongoing Cold War, which had heated up in 1959 with the Nixon-Khrushchev Moscow "kitchen debate" and Fidel Castro-led Cuban revolution.

"Will we run and hide, bury our heads in selfishness and disdain, when the visible head of that Body, which is the Church, begs our prayers and the most generous gift of our purses?

"Say, 'Lord, I am my brother's keeper.' Say it with your prayers and the token of your belief and love of God — by a substantial gift from your pocket — to aid the Church in her anxiety to outstrip Communism in the struggle for mankind's soul."

(A selection of additional "Mission Chats" columns can be found in the appendix.)

Chapter Six

Recollecting a Brother Priest

In September of 1950, Rome honored Father Anthony Brouwers by bestowing on him the title of "Chaplain to His Holiness," the first rank of monsignor. Nine years later he would be named "Prelate to His Holiness," the next rank of monsignor. Both papal designations, which carry the title Reverend Monsignor, are based on a number of criteria. But, primarily, the cleric must have led an "exemplary" priestly life. Moreover, he had to be recognized by fellow priests for outstanding pastoral ministry and leadership.

The six men interviewed here knew Tony Brouwers not only as a brother priest. True, he celebrated the Eucharist and other liturgies with them, and even on occasion heard some of their confessions.

But they also swapped episcopal war stories, played golf and tennis, and shared meals together. Some saw him as an older and wiser mentor, who knew the chancery bureaucracy as well as the '56 Ford he loved to tinker with. Others lived with him in rectories or worked with him at the archdiocese's headquarters and parishes. One senior priest was even his contemporary, going back as far as being classmates in the junior seminary.

Monsignor Brouwers also helped foster the arts among area Catholics.

Recollecting a Brother Priest

All called him a friend, however, as well as a man of God.

"We were in Los Angeles College, the old junior seminary, together, which is now Daniel Murphy High School. He was a real smart guy, oh sure. Used to slip me homework and say, 'You want a copy, Ozzie?' He knew Greek and Latin, and some other modern languages. He read a lot," recalled Monsignor Francis Osborne a few months before he died in January 2004.

"Tony had a good sense of humor and liked to joke around. I think that was his nickname: 'Hey, joker!' And he was a good football player. I played quarterback and ran the team. He was a tackle, who liked to compete. But he wasn't a braggadocio. No, he was a very humble person," the then-91-year-old priest said before adding with a straight face, "There aren't many of us, you know."

The two adolescent seminarians, who both attended Sacred Heart Elementary School and were ordained in 1938, remained friends throughout their lives. Monsignor Osborne estimated that they must have played 700 to 800 rounds of golf together over the years.

"He was a good priest, a spiritual man," the longtime pastor of Our Lady of Grace parish in Encino stressed. "And if he were alive now, I'd go to confession to him. I would. I think that God gave him the grace, like he gives everybody. It's up to us to accept that grace and put it into practice. And Tony did that."

When it came to the missions, Monsignor Osborne was one of many priests to describe his golfing buddy as a "visionary."

"He used to talk about Africa and South America — well, the whole world — and how we had been ordained for the whole world, not just for one little section of it," the priest reported. "And he wanted to send lay men and women to them because he said salvation is destined for not just priests or bishops and cardinals.

"That was a radical thing back then, but Cardinal McIntrye was for it," he pointed out. "Still, there were some who didn't want lay people sent to the missions. So Tony had to really fight to keep it going. But he was a good fighter, too. A visionary and a fighter."

In Love with His Faith

Monsignor Lawrence Donnelly got to know Monsignor Brouwers when both men lived at St. Agnes parish from 1949 to 1953. The former, just out of

In February 1953, Monsignor Brouwers enrolls first-graders in the Holy Childhood Association.

the seminary, was a 20-something associate pastor who taught at a nearby Catholic high school. The latter, who had recently been named archdiocesan director of the Propagation of the Faith, was in-residence at the urban Los Angeles parish near Vermont Avenue and West Adams Boulevard.

The young Father Donnelly and another associate pastor lived on the second floor of the rectory, with Monsignor Brouwers one floor above them. After putting in long days at the chancery and numerous evening meetings with mission groups, the director would still stop by to talk when he finally got back home.

"Usually, he'd have a cigarette and he'd be sort of dragging because it would be late, ten o'clock or so. He'd either have Propagation of the Faith work, or he'd be with Bishop Manning at some ceremony," the retired priest remembers. "But he'd always poke his head in our rooms and talk about things — and always something funny and joyful. It was something we looked forward to every evening."

Over the four years, Monsignor Donnelly believes he got to know Monsignor Brouwers "pretty well." He watched him fix toasters and lamps in the rectory, and work on his Ford during days off. Studied the sacred way the seasoned priest celebrated Mass and benediction in the church. Sought his advice on personal as well as clerical matters. Marveled at his astute observations. And laughed at his jokes and stories, often told in a dead-on mimicking voice.

"Bishop Manning would always come by and pick him up for a ceremony," he says. "We might be still at the table for lunch, and they were going to go to a confirmation on a Sunday. And Tony would look out the windows and he'd say, 'I'm looking to see if *the kid* was here yet,' because he was only a couple years younger than Bishop Manning.

Grinning now, Monsignor Donnelly adds, "So every once in awhile, we would say when we'd see him getting ready to go, 'Is *the kid* here yet?'

"And Tony would say, 'Don't let him hear you say that.'"

But the thing that impressed the young associate the most was Monsignor Brouwers' bedrock faith and vehement sense of evangelization.

"Tony just had such a love for the faith," he says. "The idea of the lay missionaries was because he was so intensely in love with the Church that he wanted other people to know about it. And he was just beginning the concept of forming them when I first met him at St. Agnes. He would sit there smoking away at the table after meals telling us what he was planning to do.

"We just listened and thought, 'This is a pipe dream. How can he ever do it?' Because it had never been done before. How was he going to convince the big man [Cardinal McIntyre] downtown? It had to involve insurance and liability for the people who would be sent for three years. I mean, religious orders took care of their own, and bishops were responsible for their diocesan priests. But what about lay people?

"So there were hurdles that we thought were insurmountable," Monsignor Donnelly adds with a shrug. Then another smile creases his face. "But we knew if anybody could pull it off, Tony could.

"He was such a holy man, and yet down to earth with a tremendous sense of humor. He could joke with the best of them and really roar with laughter. A very joyful man. And a manly fellow who could take care of his car, but also very spiritual. There was just something so precious about him."

Continuing the Incarnation

Monsignor John Sheridan became close to Tony Brouwers in the early '50s, when he was appointed chaplain of the Catholic Information Center in downtown Los Angeles. The Irish priest would invite missionaries to the center almost every week, which was a bustling place with seven Masses on weekdays and a dozen on holy days.

The director of the Propagation of the Faith would come to 809 South Flower Street to visit with these men and women who literally carried the Gospel to the four corners of the planet. And starting in 1955, when the first group of Lay Mission-Helpers was being trained, Monsignor Brouwers held classes for the lay missioners and celebrated liturgies with them at the center.

Over the 14 years Monsignor Sheridan ran the Catholic Information Center, he got to know and appreciate the erudite churchman.

"Tony Brouwers was just a truly wonderful priest, and had a very keen theological sense," he says. "He had the theological sense that he saw the Church in the vast perspective of history. And he saw evangelization and missionization in the context of the continuation of the Incarnation — of projecting the life, death and resurrection into the lives of people, helping them to grow, really, in knowledge of and relationship with Christ.

"And Tony also saw the vast problems in terms of Christology, because Christianity has only reached a small segment of the human family even at this point. So, in a marvelously developed spiritual sensitivity, Tony wanted to spread the Word and to spread the Gospel, and do both at home and abroad."

Monsignor Sheridan, pastor emeritus of Our Lady of Malibu parish, says he got to know the priest's theology as well as anyone.

"You see, Tony's interest in the missions began with an interest in what we call evangelization," he explains. "He never disconnected the foreign missions as people tended to do from the mission at home. In other words, he saw the continuity.

"But others downsized the idea of going abroad: *Why get involved over there to spread Western ideas and all that.* Members of the hierarchy were concerned about how you really presented the Lord Jesus within the framework of a whole different culture where they practiced all kinds of religious beliefs that we call superstitions."

The priest's global theology also led him to another ahead-of-his-time conviction, according to Monsignor Sheridan, that the Church needed to use the most modern means of communication available to reach people. Besides his column in *The Tidings,* he even had a local weekly radio show for a few years and tried hard to establish an archdiocesan media commission. With a small smile, the retired pastor recalls Monsignor Brouwers saying more than once that if St. Paul were around today "he would have a microphone in his hand."

But, at the time, Cardinal McIntyre was far more interested in building schools and churches than in establishing some state-of-the-art ecclesiastical communication system. So the priest's attempt to organize a media commission fell on deaf ears at the chancery.

With two brothers, Farrel and Pat, who were Holy Ghost Fathers and missionaries in Nigeria and Kenya, Monsignor Sheridan says he knows what made up the heart and soul of these modern day apostles — and Tony Brouwers had those same spiritual stirrings. He was that rare diocesan priest, in short, with a missioner's mind-set.

"He didn't separate our Church in America from the Church in Third World countries," he stresses. "And that showed the kind of cosmic thinking of this man. It's individuals like the great Karl Rahner and Tony Brouwers who were at heart missionaries as well as being theologians.

"We have this old expression in Latin, *centera coma ecclesial,* to think with the Church or feel what the Church really means," Monsignor Sheridan adds. "And Tony had that."

Monsignor O'Leary, third director of the L.A. Propagation of the Faith, visits Papua New Guinea.

Idealist and Salesman

Monsignor Lawrence O'Leary was a first-year theology student at St. John's Seminary when he met Monsignor Anthony Brouwers. Elected by fellow seminarians as the school's mission director, the young man was in charge of "Mission Day" that fall, and the Propagation of the Faith director was, of course, an honored guest.

In September 1953, after he was ordained and working at All Saints parish, the new priest was assigned to be a notary one day a week in the Marriage Tribunal at the chancery downtown. He would hear other priests talking about Tony Brouwers and his international ministry. Later on, he would chat with him during coffee breaks and lunch.

"All I knew of him was that he revolutionized the Mission Office," Monsignor O'Leary says. "It was kind of dead in the water, you know, run by directors who only worked part time at it. The only thing they ever did was send out collection envelopes every year on Mission Sunday. But he began to organize Mission Circles at parishes to support the missions. And he would go out at night to talk to these groups throughout the archdiocese.

"He also started the Mission Cooperative Plan, where missionaries from all over the world could come here and preach in churches and take up a collection for their particular diocese. He resurrected the Holy Childhood Association for parochial school kids to support the missions. He energized the whole thing."

Then in 1956, when he was an associate pastor at Our Lady of Loretto parish, Father O'Leary read a story in *The Tidings* that truly amazed him. Monsignor Brouwers, with the blessing of Cardinal McIntrye, had started a program called the "Lay Mission-Helpers" to send ordinary lay men and women to Catholic missions around the world every year. No other U.S. diocese or religious denomination had ever done anything like that before.

The young priest was genuinely impressed and three years later thrilled when he was named assistant director of the Mission Office.

And that is how in 1960 he found himself shoehorned into the cab of a pickup with Monsignor Brouwers and a mechanic named Leonard, driving on single-lane rough roads and dodging bandits to visit lay missionaries in Nigeria, Ghana, Zimbabwe and other African nations. During the month-long trip, he learned firsthand about the poverty of the Third World as well as a lot about his own supervisor.

"I found out that Monsignor Brouwers spoke Dutch," says the pastor emeritus of St. Martin of Tours parish in Los Angeles with a chuckle. "I never knew that, but there he was conversing with Mill Hill Fathers in Dutch. And I saw that he was not a well man. His back was really bothering him, so he couldn't drive. The travel was difficult for him, and he looked so haggard. At the time, he was only in his late '40s. I think he knew that he had only so much time, so he really wanted to see Africa this time by land. He had purchased and shipped over to Capetown this Ford pickup, which showed another side of him.

"Monsignor Brouwers was an idealist, but not practical in some ways," the priest notes. "The truck would have an unhappy life because it was American and they had no parts for it over there. It was also a big gas guzzler, when everybody else had these little trucks that got 50 miles to the gallon. The people in towns would take a look at it and they'd know it belonged to some American."

Monsignor O'Leary says the director also took an idealized view of some Lay Mission-Helpers, sending inexperienced men and women on assignments they could not handle because of cultural differences and personal factors. And his boss could be "tough" on those lay missioners who did fail, returning home to the states before their three-year hitch was up.

"He was a tremendous salesman who had the ability to force a round peg into a square hole," the retired priest points out. "Or vice-versa. He would make people think that they were the greatest person in the world and that they could do anything: *'Your talents are so great and so needed, and you'll have no problem whatsoever when you get to this place.'* But they'd go over there, and some of them collapsed."

Monsignor Brouwers' qualities, however, made up for these proclivities.

"He was very human, but there was also a saintly side to him," Monsignor O'Leary says. "He was a man of prayer. He had a deep faith. He had a real zeal for the Church. And he could talk endlessly, he was so enthused with his mission work. His whole being was in it when he spoke. He engaged people because they could see he was so sincere.

"And even with that dark shadow of cancer looming over him for years, he was always very active. There wasn't a lazy bone in him. By 1959, he was also pastor at St. Paul's — where he built a new parish school — on top of his full-time job at the Propagation of the Faith. And like a true Dutchman, every doorknob at St. Paul's gleamed, which tells you something about a person, too. Plus, he had his 'Mission Chats' column in *The Tidings* for I don't know how many years.

"But, more important than all these things he did, Monsignor Brouwers was a very spiritual man," his former coworker reports. "He talked about it and about theology. He loved to celebrate Mass. This was before the Vatican II Council, and he was a priest of his day."

The avid reader, amateur car mechanic, moving public speaker, clever columnist, tightfisted administrator and sometimes impractical idealist was one other thing, according to Monsignor Lawrence O'Leary. A man of vision.

The 'Punk' and the Monsignor

"I was a young punk, and he was a big monsignor."

After his grin almost disappears, Monsignor August Moretti, pastor of Assumption of the Blessed Virgin Mary parish in Pasadena, explains how he came to know and admire Monsignor Brouwers.

Shortly after his family immigrated to Southern California from Italy in 1949, he entered St. John's Seminary, having already started his studies for the priesthood in his native country. The following summer, he was working in the chancery, organizing the growing number of blueprints for churches, schools, parish halls and convents going up under the watchful eye of Cardinal McIntyre. And whenever August had a question about which plans fell into which category, "I'd go to Tony," who spoke Italian from his own years as a seminarian in Rome.

Four years later, when Father Moretti was ordained, celebrating his first Mass at St. Therese Church in Alhambra, Monsignor Brouwers preached the homily. During the next decade, the "punk" followed the monsignor's career at the Propagation of the Faith as best he could. Every time a missionary came to a parish where he was assigned or he read a newsletter from the Mission Office, the young priest would chuckle: "Oh, it's Tony again."

"We were not pals because of our age difference," the San Gabriel Valley pastor admits. "But from the way he dealt with me occasionally, I could see that he was really a man of God — and I qualify him as a true priest of the people. Very welcoming and very open, very sympathetic and very helpful. He was of great help with my mother, who didn't speak English. I would take her to Tony to have her confession said.

"He had this wonderful sense of making you feel welcome. He could be a friend at the first meeting. That's the way he struck me, anyway. Even though I was just getting my feet wet, he treated me very pleasantly and with respect. And he was a man of a good degree of erudition. He spoke a couple of languages.

"So my recollection of him as a seminarian and young priest is really admiration," he adds. "I only wish I had more personal contact with him."

Monsignor Moretti, who became a canon lawyer, remembers talking to Monsignor Brouwers about the Lay Mission-Helpers. It was a daring act not only for the volunteers, but also for the man who conceived of this "new invention."

"Because he did not find immediate approval from the hierarchy," the veteran churchman explains. "I heard that he had opposition — that there were obstacles for Tony — but I was not in the loop to know the specifics. America hasn't given birth to too many religious organizations. You think of the Vincentians from France, you think of the Jesuits from Spain, you think of the Franciscans from Italy and so forth.

"And this was a brand new thing, an association of lay people, which before Vatican II was formidable. But he himself was a missionary. I mean, his priesthood was centered on spreading the *good news* of the Gospel. And not only by encouraging priests and sisters who were already missionaries, who have a vow of religious life, but through lay people, who gave at least three years of their life.

"That takes quite a bit of convincing — and grace," Monsignor Moretti observes. "Because I don't think you can do that vocation, whether it's perpetual for life or temporary, on your own. It's a gift of God. And Tony made himself an instrument of conveying this appreciation for a temporary vocation like it was a lifelong vow."

'Christ in the People'

In the summer of 1959, Cardinal McIntyre appointed Monsignor Anthony Brouwers pastor of St. Paul Church in Los Angeles. So besides directing the Society for the Propagation of the Faith, the priest was now supposed to also run an urban parish. It would have been a Herculean task for any healthy priest in his prime, never mind an increasingly frail man of 46.

But the solution was already at hand.

Father Richard Murray had been at St. Paul's since the late '40s. The outgoing associate pastor had been secretly running the parish for three years, in fact, after the pastor became seriously ill. The congregation might have been unaware of this, but the powerbrokers down at the chancery, of course, knew the real pastoral goings-on. And so did Tony Brouwers.

Retired Monsignor Murray still remembers the first conversation he had with the new pastor:

"When he came, I wasn't talking to a stranger but a casual friend. And he said, 'I'm going to be gone a lot, if you don't mind? So you'll be practically running the parish. Any problems, you solve them. If not, hold them until I get back.'

"I said, 'Tony, I've been doing that for a couple years now.'

"He said, 'I know, good! So you make the decisions, and I'll back you up.'

"That made him feel comfortable," the priest says. "And we never had a single problem. I felt a special obligation to work hard and really put forth an effort and to keep him informed. I know it sounds like baloney, but I loved being able to help him."

The two men, along with another priest, lived in the rectory for the next three years. They ate together and celebrated Masses and feast days as a close-knit clerical team. They baptized babies, heard confessions and rushed out on sick calls. And when there was time, of course, they talked shop about the archdiocese and St. Paul's.

"Tony was very easy to get along with," Monsignor Murray says. "When he was in town, if he wasn't going out at night to a meeting, we'd be eating dinner together. It was a pleasure to be at table with him. He had lots of stories about the missions and his travels."

And the priest chuckles.

"I remember a famous expression of his. Dinner went on for quite awhile one evening, and I think he was real tired. He said, 'It's time for all good priests to be in bed.' Strange that I would remember that. He used it a couple of times. But he worked long hours. The missions weren't just a big part of his life. In fact, they were *everything*. He was going to Africa and the South Pacific, and then when he was home to all these Mission Circle meetings.

"I think he was a very strong guy, and he didn't back off because he was sick. The important thing was his work. Work was more important than his health."

Monsignor Murray thinks he knows why.

"He just loved people. He loved them here, and he loved them in Africa," he explains. "So I'm sure when he saw a need over there, it just struck a good chord. Some people are like that. And that was Tony.

"But it was even more than serving people in need," adds Monsignor Murray. "The spiritual life of the lay missionaries and doctors were vital, too. It wasn't like they were just getting a bucket of water or medicine for these people. They were getting a bucket of water for Christ — Christ in the people."

Chapter Seven

'God's Peace Corps'

In 1954, the U.S. Supreme Court handed down its historic Brown v. Board of Education decision, declaring that segregated schools deny black Americans the 14th Amendment's equal protection. The U.S. Senate censured one of its own, Joe McCarthy, for abuse of power after his five years of vicious accusations and subcommittee hearings failed to uncover a single Communist. And more than four million births occurred in the country for the first time, with the postwar baby boom continuing to top that record for the next 10 years.

A practical polio vaccine discovered by Dr. Jonas Salk was produced. Ray Kroc took over a San Bernardino hamburger stand, with the dream of franchising the fast food restaurant. And once-popular radio shows like "The Amos 'n' Andy Show" and "The Shadow" faded from the dial, while "The Adventures of Rin Tin Tin," "Lassie" and "Father Knows Best" became instant hits on TV.

Monsignor Brouwers made four trips to Africa.

In Los Angeles, Simon Rodia, an Italian immigrant tile setter and stonemason, finished the Watts Towers, which he had started working on back in 1921. Single-handedly, he raised the discarded steel frameworks reinforced with chicken wire and cement, then decorated the surfaces with bits of glass, tile, shell and pottery salvaged from railroad tracks, alleys and vacant lots. "I had in mind to do something big, and I did it," Rodia explained.

Monsignor Anthony Brouwers, the son of immigrants, was also destined to do *something big* that year, although he probably did not have a clue what it was on a Sunday morning in mid-November when he boarded an American Airlines plane with Cardinal James Francis McIntyre and four other priests at Los Angeles International Airport. Their ultimate destination was Lagos, Nigeria, where the cardinal, as Pope Pius XII's papal legate, would preside at the all-Nigeria Marian (dedicated to Mary, the Blessed Mother) Congress, officially bringing to a close the Marian Year on December 8.

The Congress took place largely outdoors at, of all places, the Lagos Race Course. It included solemn pontifical Masses, religious pageants — including a living Rosary composed of thousands of people — conferences for priests and nuns, and a closing torchlight procession and Mass, with the California cardinal delivering a personal message from the Holy Father to more than 100,000 Africans.

On his return to Los Angeles, Cardinal McIntyre declared the four-day event a resounding success. "The Congress was a great manifestation of the successful labor of the bishops, priests and sisters of Nigeria, particularly in the past 30 years," he told *The Tidings*. "They have made a great contribution to the nation, not only spiritually, but socially and economically as well."

But Monsignor Brouwers, who stayed behind to make a 90-day tour of the missions, would be struck by a radically different observation.

'We Can't Do it Alone'

The priest quickly discovered that priests, sisters and brothers were spending more of their time on secular than religious matters. And then there were the sheer numbers he could not get out of his head, which he would stress repeatedly in future talks and articles. Only 26,000 local and foreign priests were ministering to some 27 million Catholics in the Third World — never mind trying to convert the billions of unbaptized in these poor, undeveloped nations.

"A tiny army of 26,000 — a mere seven percent of the world's Catholic clergy — has the task of winning two-thirds of mankind for Christ!" Monsignor Brouwers wrote in the *White Fathers* (Missionaries of Africa) missions magazine shortly after returning home in February of 1955. "And with all their priestly duties they are burdened with a thousand non-priestly chores and preoccupations. At this rate the conversion of the world is a physical and statistical impossibility!"

In the article, he pointed out that while American Protestant denominations send thousands of missionaries out every year, there were just a "bare handful" of U.S. Catholics serving in mission lands. As proof, he cited a story in the July 16, 1956, issue of *Newsweek* reporting that of the 2,150 Christian missionaries who would leave the United States for foreign lands during the next three months, only 150 were Catholic.

"No wonder then that more and more of those specially dedicated to the Mission Cause," he observed, "realize how urgently needed are tens and even hundreds of thousands of competent and right-minded lay men and women in a worldwide ARMY of lay missionaries.

"We have waited and talked over the matter long enough," he pointed out. "Time does none of these. Neither do the enemies of Christ and the Church."

But even before his trip to Africa, Monsignor Brouwers was using his *Tidings'* "Mission Chats" as a soapbox to champion the laity cause. In the weekly's August 27, 1954, issue, he pointed out that Our Lord's legacy to the Church was to convert the entire human race. "Today, more than in ages bygone, a wholehearted sacrificing and well-trained laity is a necessity," he wrote. "A new age of mission love and sacrifice is dawning. With the terrifying shortage of priests and religious vocations in the world, an army of lay missionaries is urgently needed."

In a six-page feature story published in the *Priest* magazine after his return to the states, he spoke directly and passionately to his brother clergy: "We can't do it alone! That is, we priests cannot win for Christ all the world, and not even our parochial territories so principally not-religious and non-Catholic, without the help of many heads and hearts and hands."

He said every priest knew how hard and time-consuming the preparation of a single convert can be. Out in the world's mission fields it was decidedly more difficult, however, typically taking a minimum of 30 to 50 hours to shepherd one individual to Christianity.

"Even while pouring the baptismal water over a convert's brow, we still wonder what more we should have done to prepare this soul for its new life in Christ and the Church," he wrote in the April 1957 issue of the magazine. "Over the years when hearing of a convert's mediocrity or total lapse, we try to fathom our inadequacies.

'God's Peace Corps'

"Think then of the whole of pagans, unbaptized — all the uncounted millions, century after century, living and dying, that are out of reach of a priest. The conversion of mankind within a few steps of our rectories, as well as the wretched masses across the seas, is scarcely begun. In 19 centuries we are but one Catholic out of every six persons on earth."

The Propagation of the Faith director leads a 1961 class of Lay Mission-Helpers and Mission Doctors.

'Now You are Ready'

For Monsignor Anthony Brouwers, the whole idea of sending out lay missioners revolved around two goals, which he stated quite clearly in a lengthy story in the January 1957 issue of *The Way* magazine. First, again, was the obvious whole matter of freeing up missionary priests, brothers and sisters from social, medical and other necessary but nonpastoral tasks so that they could concentrate on their religious priorities.

"By supplying each of our missionaries with several lay men and women, trained, ready and able to stand at their sides for work that is to be done, we shall multiply their efficiency both spiritually and materially, lengthen their lives and increase their usefulness for the glory of God and the salvation of souls," he pointed out.

The second reason, however, was more sublime. It had to do with the fact that every Catholic shared through the sacraments of baptism and confirmation the "privilege duty" to help the Church convert humanity to Christ's truth and way.

Later, in a story in *The Shield* magazine, the priest described what had been driving him the past few years. "I returned to Los Angeles in early 1955 resolved to do what one could to recruit, train and assign lay men and women for short terms as volunteer helpers to missionary bishops," he wrote.

It did not take the energetic cleric long to turn his resolve into reality. By March of that year, he had already assembled and was starting to train the first class of lay missionaries who were dubbed "Lay Mission-Helpers," hyphenated to stress their signature *helper* role. They ranged from twins, who were professional Hollywood musicians, to a physical therapist and nurse to an aeronautical engineer and his new wife to a veteran photojournalist.

Two-hour classes to be held three times a week were quickly designed to get American middle class candidates spiritually, mentally and culturally ready for a drastically simpler — and harder — lifestyle. The plan called for Monsignor Brouwers and others to present 600 total hours of instruction in theology, ascetics, apologetics, liturgy, Church history, the life of Christ, scripture and missiology as well as sociology, first-aid and the history of specific missionary regions. The curriculum also included talks by visiting missionaries, who gave firsthand accounts of their experiences.

After 16 months of this diligent preparation (later reduced to nine months), candidates, as their last activity together, would go on a closed retreat before making their final decision to become lay missioners.

When Cardinal McIntyre — in spite of serious misgivings from other chancery officials — gave his approval to a constitution, rule of life, contract and schedule of classes, the Los Angeles lay missionary program was officially up and running. In July, he canonically erected the Lay Mission-Helpers Association as a "pious association" of the Catholic Church.

And a year later, on July 4, 1956, in St. Vibiana's Cathedral, the cardinal received the solemn promises of the first 10 Lay Mission-Helpers, six of whom were sent in pairs to the Sudan, Tanganyika and Nigeria. Kneeling, the two men and eight women said they would use their abilities and talents to serve the Catholic Church in the missions. The new Lay Mission-Helpers,

Dave and Kathleen Braun receive their
LMH insignia rings from Cardinal McIntyre
at a 1965 commissioning ceremony.

who ranged in age from 24 to 30, promised to serve a minimum of three years in their assigned territories.

The Church was in an expansive moment in history, and as she flourished her needs increased, Cardinal McIntrye told them. Religious missionaries could no longer keep up with this growth and still concentrate on their primary purpose. But the Church, under the inspiration of the third person of the Trinity, had come up with a solution — the laity.

"What you are doing today, while simple, has great magnitude because of the intensity of dedication, depth of love and purpose of sacrifice," he declared, commending the Lay Mission-Helpers to the guidance of the Holy Ghost and placing them under the protection of the Blessed Mother. "She will watch over you. God will be with you."

After blessing the lay missioners, Monsignor Brouwers simply said, "Now you are ready."

A Constitution and Rule of Life

The original Lay Mission-Helpers Association's constitution consisted of a preamble and 11 articles covering objectives and organization; ideals and life of members; work and activities; membership, missionary life and support; missionary service, termination and dismissal; governing of the volunteers in their missionary work; title and motto of association; patrons and canonical establishment.

According to Monsignor Brouwers, the most important duty of the lay missionaries was captured in article I: "The first objective of the Lay Mission-Helpers ever must be their own spiritual perfection and growth in holiness. Without this, all other objectives and labors in missionary fields shall be of little or no value before God and Holy Church."

The seven-page "rule of life" specifically spelled out the daily spiritual requirements of a Lay Mission-Helper in the field.

Members were expected to not only pray upon rising and before going to bed, but during their secular jobs, too. Throughout the day, short ejaculatory prayers ("God Help Me!"), the Angelus and visits to the Blessed Sacrament near the tabernacle were urged. And whenever possible, Lay Mission-Helpers were expected to attend daily Mass and receive communion. Fifteen minutes before Mass was to be spent in mental prayer and 15 minutes after communion in silent thanksgiving, renewing one's dedication to the mission cause.

Workers in the field were also urged to make the Stations of the Cross as well as to read a half-hour of Holy Scripture or spiritual literature "to stock mind and memory with the thoughts and things of God." Before going to bed, a brief but serious examination of conscience was recommended along with a heartfelt recitation of the Rosary. Weekly confession was advised, too, along with a required annual retreat of several days.

Monsignor Brouwers stressed that the Lay Mission-Helper's objective was sacred, and except for divine grace obtained from these religious practices, it could never be achieved.

But there was another purpose for all this spiritual activity, which was carefully spelled out in the rule: "As you more perfectly identify your whole life with Jesus Christ, you will become light to illumine the path of pagans and unbelievers. . . . You will thus become even more effectively a witness for Christ. Quick minds and keen eyes will be watching you constantly in the mission. You are a witness, someone showing others what they can or should be."

Lay Mission-Helpers, in short, were supposed to strive to be saints.

"Unless a lay man or woman earnestly desires sainthood and his or her lay missionary term as the means, temporary or lifelong, to gain that sainthood, he or she is ill prepared for success," Monsignor Brouwers wrote in *The Shield*, Vol. XII. "Lay missionaries are not just going overseas to build schools, repair cars, nurse the sick, teach children and write for newspapers. They are not just Catholics working in mission lands. They are first of all witnesses for Christ, with thousands of critical eyes watching their every action, appraising their every word, and seeing that lay men and women can and do live the same high ideals as their clerical and religious associates."

Lay missionaries had to witness — literally show off — Christ by their own personal spiritual lives. Neglect of minimum daily prayers and exercises was considered serious enough grounds for dismissal from the program.

Although they swore no vows, Lay Mission-Helpers promised to solemnly fulfill the spirit and word of their constitution and rule. They pledged to obey their director and overseas mission superior. Probably most amazing, however, these spiritual pioneers professed to be nothing less than holy, directing all their labors to eternal ends. What their director liked to describe as being "supernaturalized."

In the early '60s, after President John F. Kennedy had fulfilled a campaign promise to send goodwill ambassadors to aid underdeveloped nations, Monsignor Anthony Brouwers came up with another catch phrase to describe the Lay Mission-Helpers: "God's Peace Corps."

Mission Doctors

In the spring of 1959, at a symposium of the Catholic Physicians Guild of Los Angeles, Monsignor Brouwers pleaded for help from the doctors.

In his tours of Third World countries, he had come across hundreds of so-called hospitals being staffed by only nurses and paramedical professionals. There was not a single physician at these stations, which ranged from primitive bush clinics to a few well-equipped healthcare facilities in the larger towns. These centers, invariably, were the sole providers of medical care for the poor, diseased and neglected people outside of government hospitals in distant cities.

Missionary bishops had begged the Los Angeles director of the Propagation of the Faith to help them recruit physicians, dentists, nurses and healthcare technicians. A few went so far as to even promise to build and equip a new hospital if he could provide volunteers to staff it.

Seven Southern California physicians, along with Monsignor Brouwers, attended the first meeting of what would become the Mission Doctors Association in May 1959. They decided that the organization's immediate task was to supply physicians and dentists to already established mission medical facilities. Their long-range objective was to provide medical workers and equipment to the missions. And, eventually, their ultimate goal was to completely staff hospitals.

"MDA's [Mission Doctors Association] purpose is to keep Catholic mission hospitals staffed with adequate men and women," the priest told *The Tidings* in a February 5, 1960, interview. "MDA's goal is to maintain a continuity of medical service to the people of a mission area.

"The whole idea of MDA is that of the Good Samaritan," he said. "We do not wish to make 'rice Christians' or 'aspirin Christians.' We wish to exemplify the law of charity. You can't make Christians of a people unless they see the law of charity in practice."

The first volunteer to be assigned to the mission fields by the Mission Doctors Association was Thomas Bain, a soft-spoken, 31-year-old Southerner from Richmond, Virginia. The physician, accompanied by his wife, Ruth, and their four children, was sent to a new 270-bed hospital in Driefontein, Southern Rhodesia, operated by a Swiss order of nuns.

When asked by a reporter his reasons for becoming a Mission Doctor, he quipped in a soft, slow drawl, "I think this is a sure way to get to heaven." Then he added, "I also feel there is a great need among backward peoples, and I think we Americans have a debt to these peoples."

Dr. Bain said he had just finished an Army assignment where he witnessed up close the misery in mission territories. "I saw missionaries overseas in situations that would appall you," he reported. "I saw a lot of poverty. I saw situations where an American doctor could have done something.

"But I think the main reason our family is going overseas is that we can set an example as a Christian family," he pointed out. "Priests and nuns can't do that."

Since the Mission Doctors Association was founded, more than 30 Catholic physicians and dentists along with their families have served in mission hospitals and clinics in Africa, Papua New Guinea, Thailand and Latin America. After an application and screening process, accepted candidates live in community with Lay Mission-Helpers preparing for the missions. During the training, which now runs from August to December, they take classes in theology, scripture, mission culture and Catholic social doctrine. Candidates then receive a mission assignment for three years.

Starting in 1997, MDA has also sponsored a shorter one-to-three-month program, where doctors and dentists work alongside others in their field who have made long-term commitments. These short-term volunteers attend a retreat/seminar instead of the four-month residential formation program.

In a paper he wrote in 1963, only months before he died, summing up the duties and day-to-day life of a Mission Doctor, Monsignor Brouwers stressed what a "rare calling" it was to serve in the mission fields. MDA volunteers were much more than medical or dental experts helping to alleviate physical suffering. They were individuals of supernatural ideals and apostolic motivation who carried with them to distant lands, despite all the hardships and inevitable disappointments, the divine figure of Jesus Christ.

And although Mission Doctors, unlike their Protestant counterparts, were not expected to be evangelists or preachers, they were supposed to exemplify the best of Christian virtues. In short, their generosity had to go beyond the humanitarian ideal of the Hippocratic oath until their souls were fired with the zeal of St. Paul.

But for those healthcare professionals brave enough to embrace the Mission Doctors calling, the rewards were truly awesome.

"In doing all this in Jesus' name and becoming the ideal missionary medic, you shall know, with your family, a joy of soul and a sublimity of living in your allotted earthly span unknown otherwise to men in this vale of tears," Monsignor Brouwers promised. "Is it not a life worth living? Is it not the highest fulfillment for the healer of bodies?"

Chapter Eight

Opposition from Two Fronts

"God's Peace Corps," however, faced stiff opposition from critics both in the Archdiocese of Los Angeles as well as from one of the leading churchmen of his day, who happened to be the U.S. director of the Society for the Propagation of the Faith.

In 1962, when Father Francis J. Weber, a couple years out of the seminary, was starting his lengthy career as archivist at the chancery, Monsignor Anthony Brouwers' career in the Mission Office was beginning to wind down. In less than a year, the priest's cancer would progress to a terminal stage, confining him to a wheelchair and, eventually, to Daniel Freeman Memorial Hospital.

Proud mother Henrietta Brouwers poses with her son and Cardinal Manning.

"I didn't know him personally," reports now-Monsignor Weber, "so I can just tell you what I observed from the outside, because I was the young kid on the block. Nobody understood what archives were all about, so I was sort of tolerated.

"Tony had the smallest office in the building. It was over against the wall and downstairs, and everybody used to wonder how he could even function in there. He was one of the people everybody liked. Very kind and gentle. I never remember seeing him upset. He was very busy, going either with Bishop Manning, as his first secretary, to confirmations or out to all the Mission Circle meetings.

Opposition from Two Fronts

"He was very devoted to missionary work," he adds. "And even after he got sick with spinal cancer, which is very painful, he kept coming into the office right down to the very end."

With a straight face, Monsignor Weber says that he has not "gotten very far" in his own clerical career, still holding down the fort as the Los Angeles Archdiocese's official archivist after 42 years. He has written, edited, translated, compiled and published over 100 manuscripts, including the *Encyclopedia of California's Catholic Heritage, Memories of an Old Country Priest, Magnificat: The Life and Times of Timothy Cardinal Manning* and the 1997 two-volume official biography of Cardinal James Francis McIntyre: *His Eminence of Los Angeles.*

The latter legendary churchman enjoyed playing devil's advocate when one of his priests came to him with a new idea, according to his biographer, which is exactly what Father Brouwers did in the early spring of 1955, when he pitched the idea of starting a bold program to train and send lay people to the missions. The one-time Wall Street tycoon would have asked the 42-year-old priest some very tough questions, especially about who was going to pay for all this.

"McIntyre probably gave him some problems at first," Monsignor Weber acknowledges. "The basic thing he'd want would be for it to be able to function independently of the diocese financially. And that was very difficult to do, which shows you how savvy Brouwers was. With over 50 Mission Circles in parishes plus individual sponsors, he realized it could be self-supporting — and it was.

"So McIntyre not only bought it, he was enthusiastic about it. Others might tell you he wasn't, but I saw the papers, and it was very clear he was enthused. He never went into anything half-heartedly. As a former stockbroker, he had a sharp financial eye and could see that this could work. So he openly backed the Lay Mission-Helpers, and even went to a few of the countries where they were stationed.

"I imagine Brouwers had some very interesting conversations with McIntyre," he adds with a quarter grin. "See, although he was always considered an archconservative, McIntyre would always listen to you. And you could change his mind if you had a good argument. I saw that happen a couple of times. And Brouwers was able to sell him, which was a big, big thing in those days."

Monsignor Weber says it also did not hurt that the cardinal at one time wanted to be a missionary himself. Before he entered a New York seminary, in fact, he had applied to be a Maryknoll priest so he could work in the missions. In addition, according to the archivist, Monsignor Brouwers had the solid support of up-and-coming Bishop Timothy Manning, a close personal friend, who would later visit the mission fields many times himself as the Archbishop of Los Angeles.

But as much as Cardinal James Francis McIntyre and the future Cardinal Manning were in favor of sending lay men and women to the missions, their second-in-command was dead-set against it.

'Gray Eminence' Raises Concerns

In 1952, after ordaining him only two years before, Cardinal McIntyre handpicked Father Benjamin Hawkes to be his personal secretary. Perhaps the cardinal, with his business background, was impressed by the young priest's own early career as an accountant at the Lockheed Aircraft Company, where he rose quickly through the ranks.

Monsignor Hawkes also advanced steadily in the chancery, being named chancellor in 1962 and vicar general five years later. He died in 1985 at the age of 66.

Cardinal McIntyre referred to him as the "concertmaster" of the Los Angeles Archdiocese. In a *Tidings* interview, he explained that "the concertmaster selects the programs, rehearses the orchestra and then steps aside for the conductor. The musicians often bristle at the concertmaster's methods, but they all respect his ability to blend their individual efforts into soothing music."

Others were less kind.

The *Los Angeles Times*, in an October 18, 1982, feature, called him the chief moneyman who controlled the purse strings of the local Catholic Church — a "legend" who wielded immense power under the two cardinals. The newspaper observed that to the more than 1,000 priests in the three-county archdiocese, he was as much feared as respected.

"I felt just like the (cowardly) lion in the 'Wizard of Oz,'" one priest, who was a principal, told the *Times* reporter about a one-on-one meeting he once had with Monsignor Hawkes. "You're just like this," he said, making a hand gesture like he was squashing an ant. "When you are vulnerable, you can be banished and sent to the desert. People are called in, and you stand in front of him and he never offers you a seat."

Monsignor Hawkes was such a formidable presence, in fact, the actor

Opposition from Two Fronts

Robert De Niro observed him saying Mass to prepare for the role of a behind-the-scenes priest-power broker in the 1981 movie "True Confessions."

"To priests and parochial school administrators who must come to him for money for their building programs, Hawkes can be an imposing figure," *The Times* declared.

There are no records in either the Archdiocese's Mission Office or archives of correspondence between Monsignors Brouwers and Hawkes in regards to the Lay Mission-Helpers. But a number of senior priests interviewed reported that the "moneyman" would have had major concerns about continuing a new church program that was fraught with legal and financial dangers.

Monsignor Weber said he was not surprised that the bottom-line-minded chancellor and vicar general — who he refers to as the "gray eminence"— would be against the idea of sending lay men and women to Third World countries. "And the reason would have been the same that McIntyre might have had concerning some hesitations — it was a tremendous liability," the archivist points out. "Because one major lawsuit could destroy everything."

"Remember now, it was a tremendously innovative thing to do," he says. "This was way back even before the Peace Corps. And here comes a little priest from Los Angeles coming up with an idea that was just too much for some of the hierarchy to fathom. The idea of sending lay people over there was new. And that was one of the geniuses of it — it just wasn't done in those days.

"Of course he was going to get opposition," Monsignor Weber stresses. "Anything you ever do that's great and new, you're going to have trouble. Because there are those who say, 'Well, we can't do that.' Now I don't know what their relationship was. But, again, it stands to reason that Hawkes would have had reservations about liability."

A priest who had the catbird seat to know what the two monsignors' relationship was actually like is Monsignor Lawrence O'Leary, who served as assistant director of the Society for the Propagation of the Faith under Monsignor Brouwers from 1959 to 1964.

The pastor emeritus agrees that the local Church hierarchy was "scared to death" of the legal and financial ramifications of sending lay people off to the missions. And he is not shy about naming the cutting-edge program's number one critic.

"Some people wanted it to die," Monsignor O'Leary reports. "The diocesan consultors, a body of priests appointed by the cardinal, thought it was crazy.

And Monsignor Benjamin Hawkes wanted it to die. Sometimes I suspect that's why they appointed me assistant director, because they thought that I would not be effective in keeping the whole thing going. There were all sorts of Machiavellian things going on. Monsignor Hawkes was always ridiculing the Lay Mission-Helpers and the work we were doing. He called us the 'Office of Travel,' always in derisive terms. And he was a very, very powerful person as far as controlling people's lives.

"Monsignor Brouwers suffered in the chancery. He felt he was being mistreated and was very frustrated. They were trying to contain him and also even accused him of misuse of money about the Lay Mission-Helpers, but they couldn't find any evidence because there wasn't any. So there was a definite push to destroy the Lay Mission-Helpers, to stop the movement."

But the priest from Lincoln Heights was no pushover.

"Brouwers was a fighter who was fighting back," Monsignor O'Leary recalls. "You know, he had a column in *The Tidings* every week, and he had the gift of writing. Plus, he was a charismatic speaker. So he'd take Hawkes and the others on. And he could outsmart them in many ways."

Head to Head with Bishop Sheen

In 1955, TV dinners were a year old, and two-out-of-three U.S. households had at least one television set. Prime-time hits included "Texaco Star Theater," "Alfred Hitchcock Presents," "Gunsmoke," "The Honeymooners," "The Lawrence Welk Show" and "The $64,000 Question."

But none of these shows were more popular than "Life Is Worth Living," which featured Bishop Fulton J. Sheen of New York talking directly to viewers about character, war and peace, suffering and, of course, God. Dressed in a black cassock with purple piping, a purple cape and skull cap, and a gold pectoral cross hanging down from his neck, he was often described as having a majestic appearance. And with his deep hypnotic eyes, inviting smile, resonant tone of voice and eloquent gestures, one reviewer wrote he was simply "telegenic."

The celebrity churchman, who received an Emmy for "Most Outstanding Television Personality" and graced the covers of *Time, Look* and *TV Guide,* was also the national director of the Propagation of the Faith, which made him Monsignor Anthony Brouwers' boss.

It was this Vatican-appointed position, in fact, that kicked off Bishop Sheen's epic struggle with Cardinal Francis Spellman, which started in 1955

Opposition from Two Fronts

and would end more than a decade later with the popular bishop's banishment from New York City.

Most of the millions collected every year by national Propagation of the Faith branches and earmarked by the Vatican for the Church's missionary work around the world came from the United States. The powerful cardinal — who would later be the subject of a book entitled *The American Pope* — wanted U.S. funds to go directly to Catholic Relief Services' program to provide free surplus food to war-torn countries in Europe. He believed the commodities from CRS, which were distributed by Catholic missionaries, were a valuable tool in gaining hungry converts to Catholicism. But the bishop boldly turned down Cardinal Spellman's request, and was later backed up by Propagation officials in Rome, who wanted to keep all collected moneys under their control.

The battle lines of defiance and duty were joined. The two famous Catholic clergymen would clash again and again over use of Propagation money until October 1966, when Bishop Sheen was ordered to give up his leadership of the Pontifical organization to become the bishop of Rochester, a backwater diocese in western New York.

Bishop Sheen waged another battle in 1955 — this one against a mere humble priest out in California — he would also lose. According to local Lay Mission-Helpers and Mission Doctors, as well as other sources, Monsignor Brouwers was still fired up from what he had learned during his three-month sojourn in Africa when he approached the U.S. director of the Propagation of the Faith about sending lay men and women to assist missionaries. And when the headstrong Bishop Sheen gave him the same answer he gave Cardinal Spellman, the Los Angeles monsignor was even more determined to send Catholic members of the laity to the missions.

"I did hear about that, it's true," retired Bishop John Ward recalls. "See, everybody didn't jump and clap when Tony came home from Africa all excited about sending out lay missioners. They just thought missionaries had to be priests, brothers or nuns. That was it.

"Sheen was undoubtedly one of our finest bishops, and was into the missions. But I could see Sheen resenting anyone else coming out leading the mission band. I don't think he would sabotage Tony's efforts, but he certainly would say, 'Well, I'm supposed to be the leader.'

"He had a pretty big ego," the bishop points out, "and Tony was on his turf."

Whereas Monsignor Brouwers saw missionary priests and religious doing a hundred tasks that lay men and women could do better, Bishop Sheen was reluctant to rely so heavily on the laity.

"I think Sheen was uncertain about their ability to do the job," observes Bishop Ward. "Also, it would disrupt the programs that were in effect, and he didn't know what it might mean down the line. He wanted to forestall any interruption of successful programs that were already in existence: *Is this going to turn everything upside down? Will lay people be able to do the job that priests, brothers and nuns are already doing?"*

Sacrosanct Funds

Monsignor Lawrence O'Leary, the former assistant director and eventual third director of the Los Angeles branch of the Propagation of the Faith, has a decidedly different take on the rift between Bishop Sheen and Monsignor Brouwers. He argues that the disagreement was more of a structural and legal matter than anything else. Because the Propagation's general fund was "sacrosanct," he says local directors could not arbitrarily draw assets out to start a new program or support some pet charity.

"All of this money was distributed by the superior council in Rome, although the money did not actually go to Rome," he explains. "It went to the New York office, and was kept in dollars there. Then the superior council told the national director to send checks for this amount to such-and-such missionary bishop or program. And in that way, the currency wasn't constantly changing, so it was not going to lose its value.

"So Fulton Sheen saying 'no' was perfectly logical," he says. "It wasn't that he was against the idea. The Propagation of the Faith constitution wouldn't allow it."

However, another factor, Monsignor O'Leary concedes, was simply a clash of personalities.

"Monsignor being the type of person he was — a real rebel — was not at all impressed with Fulton Sheen," he reports. "In fact, he didn't care for him. I think what he didn't care about was that Sheen wanted to control everything, and, of course, Monsignor Brouwers was the same way. But the national director of the Propagation of the Faith couldn't tell bishops what to do and what not to do. So, within a diocese, if a man wanted to start a project to send lay people overseas, he could. But he had to raise the money himself, which is exactly what Monsignor did.

Opposition from Two Fronts

"Fulton Sheen raised a lot of money because of his gifts and charisms. You never missed his TV show. He was an actor and a very holy man. He had a brilliant mind and profound sense of theology, and he could translate it into common English and make it understandable. He always ended his talks about his 'lepers' in Africa. I think this, in part, gave Monsignor Brouwers the idea of going to Africa. It was his example.

"But Fulton Sheen," he adds, almost smiling now, "was also full of himself."

Betty Risley served three stints as a Lay Mission-Helper in Nigeria, Cameroon and American Samoa. During her 1961-62 training on Wednesday and Friday evenings and Sunday afternoons, she remembers Monsignor Brouwers explaining the now familiar story about how the whole program started.

The former college professor clearly recalls another thing Monsignor Brouwers talked about during his well-prepared lectures on the history of the lay missionary program and how it deeply troubled her — the opposition he received from none other than Bishop Fulton J. Sheen.

"Well, I remember him telling us about how when he came back from the tour of Africa he was very interested in sending lay people over there," she says. "He really thought that that was important because it was a big gap in the missions. So he approached Fulton Sheen, who was at the time the national head of the Propagation of the Faith, and everybody watched him on TV. But Bishop Sheen said it was not necessary to send lay people. He couldn't see any purpose in sending lay people to the missions.

"I think that Monsignor Brouwers was very disappointed. I think he just saw Sheen as somebody who didn't have vision. But he was not one to let somebody stand in the way of what he had made up his mind to do. Oh, he was very energetic, very dynamic, very determined. He really felt that this was necessary, and had the attitude, *'I don't care who's against this — even Fulton Sheen.'*

"That probably was just enough to spark Monsignor," the veteran Lay Mission-Helper adds with a knowing smile. "He was going to find a way to do it. And he did. I mean, how many of us did he train and send into the missions?"

Chapter Nine

Teacher, Motivator, Visionary

Since 1956, more than 700 Lay Mission-Helpers and Mission Doctors have served in 35 countries around the world. Frances Laterza was a member of that first class to be sent overseas.

A year earlier, the 31-year-old single woman had met Monsignor Brouwers when she applied to the Los Angeles Archdiocese's new lay missionary training program. At the time, she was teaching physical therapy at Children's

Monsignor Brouwers runs the projector after a 1960 Christmas dinner in Long Beach.

Hospital of Los Angeles and told the priest straight-out that she just wanted to learn more about her Catholic faith. There was no way she could go off to the missions because she was taking care of her widowed mother. That was totally out of the question.

"We must have had classes for a year-and-a-half at St. Agnes parish before the first group actually went," Laterza recalls. "And the more I heard him, it just seemed as if everything was kind of coming this way, and then I just had to go.

"He was very, very spiritual. For most of my life up to that point, I'd been a nominal Catholic. As children, we didn't go to church, so I had an awful lot to learn.

Teacher, Motivator, Visionary

But it was really great. I remember one of the things he would say during the class: 'If you're trying to get away from something, like a job you don't like or a bad relationship, remember you have to take yourself with you.' I thought about that many times. But there just wasn't anything that I wanted to do after that."

In late December of 1956, she was sent to Chala, Tanganyika, in East-Central Africa to work with the Medical Missionaries of Mary, an Irish order of nuns. She did a little bit of everything at the village hospital, including digging graves and whitewashing outhouses, in the remote bush mission, which had no electricity or running water. The young woman, who was born and raised in Massachusetts, however, spent most of her time assisting with surgeries in the hospital, giving anesthetics. Night operations were done by the light of kerosene lamps or car lights.

Fran Laterza, a physical therapist, volunteered in Tanganyika.

"I liked everything at Chala and the other mission I was transferred to," Laterza says. "The people were quite nice. They didn't understand us. For example, I wore hosiery. Some of the people would come up to me and touch the stockings, because they had never seen them before."

She adds, "But everything was interesting," grinning. "We made a great effort to learn Swahili, and even now I can understand some of it. But there's a universal language, and you can almost tell if people like you or don't like you. I never had any fear, even when I was called to go down to the hospital in the middle of the night. Oh, the snakes might have frightened me a little bit, but I ended up killing about 17 of them, cobras and others."

In the early '60s, when Laterza returned to the states for the final time, after two tours in Africa, she continued working with Monsignor Brouwers through the Mission Circles. She begged doctors and drug stores for samples of aspirin, penicillin and bandages to send to missionaries. Twice she was in charge of all the Missions Circles, which numbered more than 100. Today, she is still involved with two circles, #81 and #114, and continues to collect medical supplies for the missions.

And during the last six months of his life, the physical therapist worked with the priest whenever he came out of the hospital to visit his parish, helping him exercise his muscles to ease the spasms.

She remembers his quick wit and how he liked to joke around. A favorite game at retreats and parties was called "Stink Pink." A player would come up with a noun modified by an adjective, which had to be matched with a synonym having the same number of syllables. For example, "chubby female" could be matched by "fatty Patty."

Monsignor Brouwers was good at the game, but Laterza says she could sometimes best him. One remark he made she has never forgotten: "Fran, I can just envision you in the presence of the Good Lord in heaven entertaining him with these 'stinky pinkies.'"

"So he did have a good sense of humor and play on words," she reports. "But his control of the English language was absolutely beautiful. The words would just come to him — really spiritual things. It was always very inspiring. When he got finished, you just wanted to go serve. And I think if you look at some of the things he's written, you'll see what a good writer he was, too.

"As a priest, he was perfect. He didn't rush through a Mass. You really could feel that he was communing with the Lord. All of his homilies were good. He could speak spontaneously. And he treated everybody respectfully."

Laterza pauses, shaking her head.

"And in class, there were some people who were at loggerheads with him. One of the fellows was sure that animals have intellect. Monsignor would say 'no,' and explain why they didn't. This man would persist and kind of needle him, but he always handled it well. And we just wanted to hit this guy.

"I think people liked him automatically," she notes. "He did have a charisma because he seemed sincere in what he was trying to do. He worked hard. He was always courteous to people. But he had to convince bishops at this time when no Catholic lay people went out to the missions that this was a good thing for them."

The 79-year-old still single woman believes Monsignor Brouwers was way ahead of most Catholic clerics on a number of issues, but none more so than the role of the laity in the modern Church.

"Everybody today seems to be asking that in time, if there's not enough priests and nuns to go around, 'Who will carry the banner?'" she muses.

"He showed that lay people can come to the fore and contribute some of their many talents.

"He would say very often that in time *we* will be the country to whom other countries send missionaries. And isn't it happening? He could see the shortage of priests and religious coming."

After a moment of silence, Laterza says, "Well, I think everybody in a supernatural way loved him. He couldn't say anything wrong, and he just inspired you to do everything for God. He's a hard one to forget."

'What I Am Today'

Addie Coronado returned from Africa a changed woman.

Addie Coronado, a member of the second Lay Mission-Helpers class, was also assigned to Tanganyika in late 1957 to work with Fran Laterza. The first impression the San Fernando Valley resident had was total culture shock: "Everybody was black."

Less than a year earlier, the obstetrics nurse had met Monsignor Brouwers at the chancery on Ninth Street, responding to a letter he wrote to the Archdiocesan Council of Catholic Nurses about a new lay missionary venture that was desperate for healthcare workers. After that, things started moving pretty fast for the then-29-year-old woman.

"I was just like overwhelmed, because he immediately said, 'Oh, you can go to Chala in Tanganyika,' and he didn't know me," she recalls with a laugh. "I thought, 'How can he say this and not really know me?' But I thought it was wonderful, too, because I'd pictured working in the missions for a long time."

When Coronado started going to the training classes, again she was impressed by this priest who so openly expressed a steadfast confidence in ordinary lay people.

"Just his character — he was so positive," she says. "And you could talk to him person to person easily, and discuss any little difficulties that you

might have or you think you might run into. But he was always like" —
and her voice softens — "'It'll be OK.' The training was a period of really
concentrating on what you were doing and what you were going to do,
and then setting your mind to just fall into whatever came.

"One thing I recall he emphasized was not to decide before you're there,"
she adds. "So I went with an open mind, and whatever I was to do, I would do."

Monsignor Brouwers traveled to Rome with the group after their training,
where they received their Lay Mission-Helpers rings, which Coronado says
was exciting. Plus, the 19 successful candidates got to interact with their
teacher and spiritual mentor outside of class, experiencing firsthand some
of what she describes as his "nonchalant" playful demeanor.

For example, one afternoon, when the men in the group had overslept
their Italian siestas, the priest decided to escort five of the young women
around Rome. As they approached a busy intersection with lots of pedestrians,
he quipped, "I'd better remove this before people start talking," reaching up
and sticking his collar in a pocket.

Later, he suggested, "Why don't you ladies go have your hair done?"
According to Coronado, they all thought this rather hilarious since they had
often been told in class that you went to the missions with only the clothes
on your back and did not worry about appearances.

She also remembers the letters the director would send the lay missionaries every month, answering their concerns and offering personal sugges-
tions. Plus, there were his regular morale trips to the missions fields, even
when he was suffering the ravages of cancer.

"He was always advocating the uplift," she says.

The veteran Lay Mission-Helper, who did three three-year tours as a
nurse and midwife in Africa, is not sure why Monsignor Brouwers loved
the missions so much. But she has a pretty good idea that it was tied to
his bedrock view that the Catholic Church was a truly universal Church,
belonging to no one country or continent. Moreover, he was a "people person," who simply wanted to help other human beings as much as possible.

As a public school kid, who was never that familiar with priests,
Coronado is reluctant to speculate on his holiness. All she knows is how
much attention he paid to each Lay Mission-Helper candidate and how
passionately he spoke of the laity.

"He made us aware that we are the Church," she says. "The Church was
ours — mine! And this was before the changes with Vatican II. There were

so many priests and nuns available at the time, the common thinking was *Why do we need anybody else to go to the missions?* But he saw us as good examples to other people. He would say you don't have to be a nun or priest to be a good Christian. So, obviously, he was way ahead of his time."

When Addie Coronado came back to the states, she was a changed woman. She went from being an apathetic Catholic, who made her first Communion and confirmation and then "went on my merry little way," to serving as a Eucharistic minister, lector, religious education teacher and minister to the elderly at Our Lady of Lourdes parish in Tujunga.

But it was not just because of what the Southern Californian had seen and done as a lay missionary. Monsignor Brouwers had left an indelible mark of inspiration. And to this day, she still communes with him, asking his advice on crucial life decisions, seeking his counsel on her own moral behavior: *"OK, Monsignor, what should I do about this?"*

"He was the seed for me going to Africa in the first place," the 76-year-old retired nurse says. "He had absolute faith in me that I could go to Tanganyika and do the job. I was just a kid, and he helped build my confidence. And, oh, yes, the time I spent there and in Kenya, and the experiences I had, made me what I am today."

'I Thought I Was Crazy'

When Lillian Casey went to Kenya as a Lay Mission-Helper, her family thought she was crazy.

Lillian Casey, who served seven terms and some 20 years as a Lay Mission-Helper in Kenya, Ghana, Israel and the United States, hoped she would die in the mission fields. Instead, she passed away at the age of 89 on February 4, 2004, while a resident of Nazareth House, a Catholic retirement and nursing home in West Los Angeles.

"Casey," as she was known to her friends, just wanted to do something for the Church when she spotted the story in *The Tidings* about the lay men and women a certain Monsignor Brouwers had trained and sent off to the missions. She had attended Santa Monica College with the goal of becoming a social worker, but wound up working in production at Douglas Aircraft. She was thinking about entering the Carmelite sisters, until she read about the six individuals who went to Africa, and immediately had a life-changing thought: *Wow! That's what I'd like to do.*

On the spur of a moment, one evening, she went to the rectory at St. Agnes parish, knowing Monsignor Brouwers lived there. "You're a hard man to meet; I've been trying to find you for months," she said. "I'm very interested in your lay missionary program."

The handsome priest just said, "Oh, you should come to our next meeting." Which she did.

"And from then on, that was it," Casey explained in a September 2003 interview.

From the very first training class, the young woman from Boston knew she had made the right decision. "I loved him," she confided with a chuckle. "Because of his personality. He was just lovable. Very outgoing and a wonderful speaker. But he was so human. Very human. And he was very humble."

She recalled the classes as being mostly long — but far from boring — lectures on spirituality. "I'll tell ya, when he talked, he'd go on and on and on," she said with an impish grin. "And we just loved it. We wished he would go on forever."

Monsignor Brouwers spoke a lot about the missions, too, and why he started the Lay Mission-Helpers in the first place. Casey remembered him also saying he wished all the trainees could live together in community (which Lay Mission-Helper candidates currently do) so that they could become "one family."

The priest even gave them an insider's view of national Society for the Propagation of the Faith meetings, where other diocesan directors would often ask in amazement, *"Where did you get that bunch of crazy people to work for the Church in the missions?"*

"Monsignor would tell us everything," she said, shaking her head. "He shared a lot of his life with us. Talked about when he was in a parish and there would be a phone call maybe two or three o'clock in the morning, somebody was dying, and how they always sent the young priest, which was him, out on these night sick calls. And he had to take a streetcar, mind you, because priests didn't have cars in those days.

"He also said that he hated getting up in the morning. He wasn't a morning person. He'd be still trying to wake up getting ready to say Mass when these

Teacher, Motivator, Visionary

little altar boys would come in so bright and cheerful: 'Good morning, Father!'" She giggled, before saying, "He was so down to earth, you know.

"And he'd read excerpts from the letters to him from people who were already in the missions. We were really thrilled. We were so gung ho about going to the missions ourselves."

But Casey's family and friends thought she was insane when she went off to Kenya in 1958. "I thought I was crazy," she said, laughing. She started an occupational school for older children, visited orphans and worked with families in outlying settlements. And almost every year, Monsignor Brouwers would pay a call. "That's why it was so successful, I think," she pointed out. "Because he visited us to find out how things were going."

Her hero died before she came home from Ghana in the summer of 1964. She knew, of course, that he was very sick, but was not aware of the details of his cancer.

The best gift the magnetic priest left behind, according to Lillian Casey, was thousands of conversions in Third World countries.

"You have no idea how many dying babies I baptized when I would visit the hospitals," she said. "He was just a wonderful man, and a man ahead of his time. And he spread goodness and love in so many people — including me."

Mission Memories

Chuck Walsh, 83, of San Diego served three tours as a Lay Mission-Helper in Papua New Guinea during the late 1950s and '60s. The former Navy storekeeper was in charge of supplies going out to missionary religious orders. When he was 36, he approached Monsignor Brouwers after reading an article in the *Los Angeles Times* about a woman from Hollywood who had volunteered in New Guinea.

"Well, it's funny you want to go out there, because I just got a letter from a bishop there who needs some help," the priest remarked.

Walsh says he was a good teacher who explained things well and inspired everybody in class. "He was very likeable," the retired postal worker points out. "He really motivated people to go to the missions because he was still fired up from what the African bishops had told him about needing people with skills.

"Well, he did change my life, and also being in the missions changed my life — especially, seeing the poverty over there," he observes matter of factly. "I don't need the material things, so I don't have to worry about living on less. But the whole experience deepened my faith. I'd like to be back there right now. Those ten years were the best years of my life. I'll never forget him."

Pat Devaney was Monsignor Brouwers' secretary before she went off to manage a bookstore in Tanzania in 1959, and worked in the Mission Office again when she returned three years later. She says he was never a demanding boss but he did have "fairly high expectations," and she worked hard to meet those. She describes him as gentle, kind and considerate, who would stop and chat every morning.

Her boss was also a generous man.

She remembers him giving the cleaning lady his new briefcase the day after she had admired it. When her own mother visited the office and commented on an African-made statue of the Blessed Mother, he gave it to her on the spot. "That was the kind of man he was," she explains. "He was always trying to free himself of material possessions."

Devaney says Monsignor Brouwers had a "great mind." Whenever he read a book, he would underline passages and jot down notes in the margins.

There was one other thing that really struck her about the priest.

"He had such a devotion to Mary — like he had a direct tie," reports the retired 79-year-old English teacher, who lives in Leisure World. "He said things that really did indicate there was direct communication from Our Lady to him."

Bill and Jean Pawek of Mountain View, California, spent two decades in the mission fields as Lay Mission-Helpers. He was a photographer and she was a botanist when they went to Malawi, Africa, in 1959, where they taught in high schools and at a teacher training college.

"I'm sure Monsignor encouraged us, or we wouldn't have stayed so long," Bill says. "But he was very inspiring and had an empathy with people. He understood each of us and would give us special advice. He did more than just lecture. Often he was talking one on one, or, in our case, to a couple. But he was doing a lot of individual counseling. The atmosphere he created in our class made it like a really big close spiritual family. He had such charisma, everything just worked well."

Jean agrees.

"He was just dynamic. I just loved to hear him talk," she says, laughing at 44-year-old memories. "He moved us so much. He talked to us about spirituality, so he had to be a spiritual person. He was so natural. He wasn't faking anything. When he talked, he just gave himself to you for that moment."

Teacher, Motivator, Visionary

Talking to God Every Night

Don Riley was leading the good Southern California life as a 20-something Hermosa Beach bachelor in the late 1950s when he got a Lay Mission-Helpers brochure in the mail. After reading it, he said to himself, "Well, I could probably do a year, but I'm sure as hell not going to do three," tossing the material aside. Six months later, when he was cleaning, he came across the pamphlet and had second thoughts.

He went to the first training session, but made no commitment, telling himself he was just checking it out. "But you talk to Monsignor Brouwers for ten minutes, you're sold," says the retired accountant today. "And after the first class, I was convinced. True story."

Stationed at the bishop's house in Malawi, Riley did accounting and bookkeeping for the local African diocese. Looking back, the Third World experience was the "best three years" the 73-year-old man ever spent. He says sending him and other lay people to Africa sounded like an ill-conceived, hair-brain idea that would never work.

"But Monsignor Brouwers was brilliant," he points out, "and a visionary." The farsighted priest also seemed close to his creator.

"In class, it was like he was talking to God every night," Riley muses. "Seriously, I mean, he just came across that way. Because when you heard him talk, you figured he had just finished talking to God and he was explaining some stuff."

The former lay missioner laughs at the recollection. But then his voice gets serious again, when he adds, "He was probably the most spiritual priest I ever met."

Paul Leehan says he became a Lay Mission-Helper in 1961 largely because of the times.

John F. Kennedy, as the newly elected president, had made his famous declaration that propelled thousands of young adults into heroic volunteerism: *"Don't ask what your country can do for you; but rather ask what you can do for your country."* The Long Beach high school teacher was one of them. But he decided to serve his Church as well as his country by working in the missions.

And he found Monsignor Anthony Brouwers just as inspiring as the charming chief executive.

"He was very down to earth, very friendly, very practical," he remembers. "He had sort of a wry, dry sense of humor and an ashen look to his face, which made me think just a few years later that, without telling us, he had been suffering a great deal. But he always seemed very even keel and positive. He knew exactly where he was going, didn't allow things to disturb him, was never on super highs or super lows."

Leehan was also affected by the director's simple lifestyle. He remembers how the long black cassock he wore to class "looked a little bit worn," as opposed to the well-dressed attire of many priests and prelates featured in glossy mission appeals of the era.

But another — more ethereal — quality impressed the teacher even more.

"There was a way about him that I did not see the other priests who were training us had," says the 68-year-old retired Spanish teacher. "They were holy in their own way. But I always felt that Monsignor Brouwers had something very unique about him. Partly it was due to his own perseverance and his sticking to the rules of the traditional game. He was very faithful to the Church.

"But also it was because he had the charism of being the founder. As the God-chosen person to found a group, he was the beneficiary of extra graces. And I have always considered it a great grace to have been in classes with him."

Dr. Herb Sorensen, his first wife, Doris, a nurse, and their three young sons had more problems than most Lay Mission-Helpers and Mission Doctors just getting to the mission fields. On their fall 1962 flight to New York, Doris became ill. After a couple of surgeries, all of a chest tumor was finally removed. The couple remained on the East Coast, nervously waiting for approval from the Mission Doctors' board to continue their long-planned trip, when they got an extraordinary telegram from Monsignor Brouwers. It read simply: "From all eternity you have been meant to be missionaries. Wiring money. Go now!"

Herb Sorensen, M.D.

Which they promptly did.

During the next three years in Malawi, the California doctor would deliver babies, do surgeries and burn grafts, work in orthopedics as well as tropical medicine. In his spare time, he helped build a mission hospital and lab plus start a nationwide organization of private medical facilities. The OB-GYN specialist would return to Africa three more times, logging some seven years there all together as a Mission Doctor.

The Sorensens were in the last training class Monsignor Brouwers was able to fully participate in before being confined to Daniel Freeman Memorial Hospital. Herb remembers him most of all as a determined individual.

"Oh, he was a purpose-driven person," he stresses. "There was no question. He had a vision. He was the only person that I have ever known who has had a vision and has been able to implement it the way he did with such tremendous complexities to handle.

"And when he talked to you, the vision that he would impart is what inspired you," the 73-year-old physician adds. "Half of the reason that we persevered overseas for three years was because he bucked us up. He gave us the same vision that he had."

Members of the Lay Mission-Helpers class of 1961 were sent to the Sudan, Nigeria, Zimbabwe, Zambia, Malawi, Ecuador, Tanzania, Saudi Arabia and the U.S.

Monsignor Brouwers has supper with Lay Mission-Helper and Mission Doctor candidates.

Lay Mission-Helpers have worked in many ministries, including producing *The African* Catholic newspaper.

Teachers have always been needed for elementary and secondary schools in the missions.

A beaming Monsignor Anthony Brouwers and Father Lawrence O'Leary get together with members of the 1960 Lay Mission-Helpers class before their departure to Ghana, Kenya, Tanganyika, Northern Rhodesia and other Third Word nations.

KENYA

TANGANYIKA

UGANDA

Greetings

Tabora, Tanganyika
Oct. 26, 1961

Your Eminence:

I have borrowed native Archbishop' Mihayo's typewriter for this missive. First I beg to report my total survival, and that all has proceeded very well up this point. Africa is not the seething continent that the world press makes it out to be. There is really nothing much to make one uneasy for the present at least. I have had no trouble healthwise, and expect none. Only the heavy rains, the unbelieveable roads and mud have slowed down progess considerably. Tomorrow however we shall escape the roads by flying to Salisbury, to visit with some 28 Lay Mission Helpers through Nyasaland and the Rhodesias, and South Africa.

While in Rome the Superior General of the White Fathers asked me to submit the medical details of my bone cancer to the Congregation of Rites, as soon as possible. Another case and mine, they believe, have the only medical history, and with the Holy Father's urging for the conclusion of the Uganda Martyrs' cause, they wish to have anything that even looks like a miracle. I have written to Dr. R. Lescoe of Los Angeles, to provide the White Father Postulator General in Rome with the medical history, and see what use is made of this instance. It does indeed feel strange to be personally a "example" for such a cause of canonization. I have also directed Dr. Lescoe to seek from Your Eminence whatever Concordat or personal remarks you may see fit to attach to his professional and medical report.

Till a later date, I am respectfully

Monsignor Brouwers used a native archbishop's typewriter to write to Cardinal McIntyre.

88

During a 1966 assignment in Zimbabwe, Lay Mission-Helper Betty Wagner is up to her neck in toddlers.

LMH teachers spend time with their students outside the classroom.

Kay Van Deudekom served as a Lay Mission-Helper in Thailand from 1973 to 1976.

Patricia Ray, a Lay Mission-Helper assigned to the Diocese of Kumbo, Cameroon, washes clothes.

Josephine DeMinville served three three-year terms in Kenya (1959, 1963 and 1982) plus an additional 1968 tour in Tanzania.

From 1981 to 1993, Lay Mission-Helper Rosella Rubel volunteered in the Diocese of Udon Thani, Thailand.

Lay Mission-Helper Jeff Matsuno visits a family in the Diocese of Makeni, Sierra Leone, during the early '90s.

Miklos Szentkiralyi (right) was a Lay Mission-Helper in Micronesia from 1975 to 2002. He died while working in the missions.

Lay Mission-Helper teachers share the joy of learning with their students.

Chapter Ten
Diagnosis and Devotion

Although he was a prolific writer and public speaker, Monsignor Anthony Brouwers was also a prudent man who rarely wrote or spoke about himself. And the normally outgoing priest was especially guarded when it came to his own welfare and health, even though he struggled with one of the most painful types of cancer for more than half a decade.

Because of this tight-lipped quality — along with the fact that his nearly half-century-old medical records are terribly incomplete — it is impossible to determine exactly when the priest's life battle with multiple myeloma actually began.

In the United States, nearly 13,000 new cases of the disease are diagnosed every year and more than 10,000 who suffer with it die, according to the National Cancer Institute. It usually strikes people over 40, while 70 is the most common age of onset. Men are almost twice as likely to develop the disease as women; African Americans are almost twice as likely to develop it as Caucasians.

Monsignor Brouwers has something to smile about with Walt Disney.

While the cause of multiple myeloma is unknown, medical researchers believe heredity as well as exposure to radiation, benzene and other solvents possibly play

Diagnosis and Devotion

a role. There is currently no cure. Treatments (including chemotherapy, radiation therapy and surgery), as they did in Monsignor Brouwers' time, focus on slowing progression of the disease as well as preventing or relieving symptoms and complications. Survival rates vary, but most MM patients die within five years of diagnosis.

Multiple myeloma starts with one abnormal plasma cell in the bone marrow, which then multiplies. But because these cells do not mature and die like normal ones, they accumulate and eventually overwhelm the production of healthy cells. Myeloma cells, which can circulate in the blood, often collect in bones — especially the ribs, spine, pelvic bones and skull — forming tumors and causing other serious health problems.

The most common symptom of bone tumors is pain caused by bone damage or tumors pressing on nerves. The pain can be as sharp as a toothache, making it hard for patients to even move. The weakened bones are highly susceptible to fractures. In addition, these damaged structures can release calcium into the blood, causing hypercalcemia.

The immune system is also compromised because myeloma cells hinder the production of normal plasma and other white blood cells. Patients have a hard time fighting off disease. Anemia is another common side effect, along with kidney problems.

Early symptoms of multiple myeloma are weakness, fatigue, pallor, weight loss and repeated infections. In advanced stages — in addition to bone pain and fractures — patients may experience severe nausea, vomiting, constipation, confusion, urination problems and weakness or numbness in the legs.

Cancer Confirmed

Ironically, Monsignor Brouwers' first self-reported cancer pain came while he was changing an exhaust pipe on his cherished Ford in June 1957. It was sudden and on the left posterior of his chest. When the area remained sore for 10 days, he consulted a chest surgeon, who diagnosed a fracture. But it did not stop the priest from pursuing another passion. Two weeks later, while moving a heavy load of books, the pain reoccurred, again lasting about 10 days.

Seventeen months later, on November 24, 1958, he reported all this to Dr. Richard Lescoe at Daniel Freeman Memorial Hospital in Inglewood, some 20 miles south of Los Angeles. The Torrance thoracic and cardiovascular surgeon performed a systemic review of his patient, including a detailed history and physical exam.

At age 11, Tony came down with whooping cough, causing a hernia that was repaired. He also had the measles. Seven years later, he fractured his left lateral Malleolus, which was still enlarged. A year later, his appendix was removed.

In 1947, while serving as Cardinal Manning's secretary, he developed hemorrhoids. Five years later, a cystoscopy (an examination of the urinary bladder) at Queen of Angels Hospital revealed a kidney stone. But he did not pass the stone until years later.

While on his first trip to Africa in 1954-'55, Monsignor Brouwers contracted malaria. He had a second attack after two months, but none since. During his four trips to the continent, he also suffered extreme diarrhea with weight loss, which was finally cured with Swiss drugs.

The physical exam revealed a well-developed, well-nourished white male "in no acute distress." He stood 5'll" and weighed 182 pounds. His blood pressure was 130 over 80. His pupils were round and equal; his thyroid was not enlarged; and his heart showed no murmurs. There were no masses or tenderness in his abdomen.

All real good news for a 45-year-old priest who smoked and was too busy for any regular exercise beyond an occasional round of golf and a couple sets on the tennis court.

Then came the bad news. An X-ray revealed a bony lesion in the posterior portion of the left 8th rib, with associated soft tissue "suggestive of myeloma." Four days later, the pathology report from a biopsy sealed the diagnosis. From tissue taken from the 8th rib, Case #S. 4084-58 showed plasma cell myeloma.

Monsignor Brouwers' post-operative recovery from the biopsy was described as "uneventful." And a skull series and spine X-rays a day later failed to reveal any secondary lesions.

Radiation therapy was begun for the patient. He received 1,700 roentgens under the direction of a Dr. Heiser, who planned to give him a total of 3,000 roentgens. He was discharged from the hospital on December 3 to Dr. Downey, his brother-in-law, for "complete care."

Dr. Lescoe ended his two-page October 18, 1961, abstract of Monsignor Anthony Brouwers' medical illness with a bit of buoyancy mixed with scientific apprehension:

"It is my understanding, that the patient had been treated by Dr. Graf

Diagnosis and Devotion

[a hematologist], following with good response. I do not know if later blood smears or bone marrow studies revealed dissemination of this disease process."

Ugandan Martyrs Cure?

An October 26, 1961, letter from Monsignor Brouwers in Tabora, Tanganyika, to his cardinal back in Los Angeles, however, showed nothing but optimism. After explaining that he had borrowed a local archbishop's typewriter, the priest on letterhead bordered with black-and-white drawings of a lion, giraffe, ostrich, elephants and zebras playfully wrote:

"First I beg to report my total survival, and that all has proceeded very well up to this point. Africa is not the seething continent that the world press makes it out to be. There is really nothing much to make one uneasy for the present at least. I have had no trouble health-wise, and expect none. Only the heavy rains, the unbelievable roads and mud have slowed down progress considerably."

Monsignor Brouwers told Cardinal McIntyre that tomorrow he would escape the bad roads by flying to Salisbury to visit 28 Lay Mission-Helpers stationed throughout Nyasaland, the Rhodesias and South Africa. Then he returned to the matter of his present good health and a startling related development:

"While in Rome the Superior General of the White Fathers asked me to submit the medical details of my bone cancer to the Congregation of Rites, as soon as possible. Another case and mine, they believe, have the only medical history, and with the Holy Father's urging for the conclusion of the Uganda Martyrs cause, they wish to have anything that even looks like a miracle."

The priest said he had written to Dr. Lescoe, who was still his physician, to provide the White Fathers' postulator general in Rome with his medical history, adding, "and see what use is made of this instance." Then the words on the African stationery almost blushed: "It does indeed feel strange to be personally an 'example' for such a cause of canonization."

Monsignor Brouwers concluded by saying he had also asked his doctor to seek from "Your Eminence whatever Concordat or personal remarks you may see fit to attach to his professional and medical report."

The "cause" of the Ugandan martyrs was a hot-button item for the Catholic Church in the fall of 1961. Upon his return to California, the director of the local Propagation of the Faith even wrote about it in the

November 10th issue of *The Tidings.* He said it was no longer a secret in Rome that Pope John XXIII had directed those in charge of the martyrs' cause for canonization to "hasten" the proceedings:

"It is the express desire of Pope John to canonize the 22 on the occasion of the opening of the Ecumenical Council late in 1962. He has expressed a personal wish that every priority be given to proving the sainthood of the Martyrs, and thus with the Council's opening, call attention to saints in the mission lands of Africa and of the place in the world which today's African peoples are assuming."

But Monsignor Brouwers had a much more personal interest in the 22 Catholic boys and young men who were killed by their native king in 1886 after refusing to renounce their new faith. Twice he had made a pilgrimage to Namugongo, where the Africans had been burned alive outside the city of Kampala — believing he had been cured of cancer through their divine intercession.

He wrote about the martyrs a number of times, including the following descriptive opening passage from a June 3, 1960, "Mission Chats" entitled "Charles Lwanga Walked Cheerfully to Martyrdom":

"It was Good Friday afternoon some weeks ago in the vicinity of Kampala in Uganda. We drove smoothly over pavement out of sprawling Kampala, watching for the turn-off to Namugongo.

"There it was, a back road of foot-deep sticky mud. Not a single sign the whole nine miles out of Kampala existed to point the way for the Christian and curious to the Shrine of the Uganda Martyrs.

"We remember that it was just 74 years before on May 26, also on a Friday afternoon at almost the same hour that Charles Lwanga and his youthful African companions were walking their way to martyrdom."

Only much later in the column — the 17th paragraph — did the priest get around to mentioning his own possible cure, in a veiled reference many readers probably missed:

"At Namugongo last Good Friday afternoon we prayed for the total conversion of Africa and thanked Almighty God through His faithful martyrs for favors received."

Pope John XXIII did not get his wish of opening the historic Vatican II Council in January 1962 with the canonization of the Ugandan Martyrs. And the following year, the jovial pontiff would himself die of stomach cancer. It was left to his successor, Pope Paul VI, to continue their cause. In his reign, during the Second Vatican Council's third session, the 22 blessed Africans were finally proclaimed saints.

Monsignor Brouwers' remission also turned out not to be a lasting cure. By late 1962, the cancer had spread to his spine, making it extremely painful for the 49-year-old man to walk or even get out of bed. In November, he was confined to Daniel Freeman Memorial Hospital, where he would reside — except for brief outings — for the last 14 months of his life.

Chapter Eleven
Caretakers

When Lay Mission-Helper Fran Laterza came back from serving in Africa in 1961, the physical therapist started working with Monsignor Brouwers as the cancer metastasized to his spine and he became more and more disabled. After her regular job, she would go to the rectory at St. Paul's to help the pastor exercise his legs to ease muscle spasms. She also remembers giving him a treatment at the annual Lay Mission-Helpers retreat at a mountain camp in Wrightwood.

An ailing Monsignor Brouwers, along with Cardinal McIntyre and Monsignor O'Leary, gather with the 1963 Lay Mission-Helpers class.

"He was struggling with paralysis in the rectory," Laterza says. "He had cancer of the bone, and he knew it. And he did have some paralysis, but he was able to kind of basically sit up. I would give him the treatments, and he'd be able to walk very laboriously with loboff crutches that go around your wrists. But then he would get tired very quickly, and I was so worried that he might fall. But, fortunately, he never did. And he even showed some signs of little strength fighting the problem of spasticity."

Monsignor Brouwers had a spastic type of paralysis, according to the lay missionary pioneer. His loss of muscle function was accompanied by involuntary contractions. With these spasms locking his muscles, he was ungainly and unstable.

Caretakers

The priest was also in considerable distress.

"It is painful because all of your nerves come out of the spinal cord and go to all parts of your body," Laterza explains. "And when you have anything wrong, even from a simple disk, you can have so much agony and pain because it involves the main center where all the nerves emanate.

"So I'm sure he must have had terrible back pain mixed with the spasms just about all the time. He would just have these horrible spasms, where he couldn't move at all. When I was trying to move his legs, I could feel the spasm. It's resistance, and sometimes it gets very painful. But his arms remained relatively strong, so that he could balance himself.

"Of course, it was hard for him because he had always been so active," she points out. "But I think he was so committed to the whole program of Lay Mission-Helpers, Mission Doctors, the Holy Childhood Association and the Mission Circles that he just wanted to give his all. Another person would possibly just lie in bed and accept it. But his disposition was such that he wanted to keep going."

The physical therapist says Monsignor Brouwers was a good role model for anyone experiencing prolonged pain. She never noticed any outward depression or mood change in her private patient. In fact, he was always quite magnanimous, greeting her with an open smile and friendly "Hi, Fran!" She is convinced he found solace in offering up his daily suffering for some greater good, possibly for the missions that had become such a major part of his priesthood.

Laterza confides it was probably harder for her. "Knowing the kind of person he was before, I really wanted to cry, but I put on a good face," she says. "I would show a little emotion: *'Good, Monsignor, that's great! Keep it up!'* But I didn't want to cry on his shoulder."

In December 1963, the priest was discharged from Daniel Freeman and moved back to St. Paul's rectory, determined to stay this time in the parish he had been pastor of since 1959. The former Lay Mission-Helper was giving him a treatment when he suddenly started sweating and said, "I guess, maybe I'd better go back." When she suggested calling an ambulance, he asked her to drive him to the hospital.

Rushing back to Inglewood, the flustered woman had to ask her patient for directions. During the drive, he said, "I just wonder if the cancer's going to my brain? The thing I worry about, Fran, is that maybe I'm losing it up here."

Laterza said, "There's no way that's happening, Monsignor," turning to her passenger. "No, I really don't see any sign of that at all." Then, trying to offer some encouragement, she said, "You know, you've got to get better because we need you. I don't think the organization can survive without you."

"If this is the work of God, it will continue and flourish; but if not, it'll die," he said. "It doesn't depend on me being around."

When they got to the hospital, Laterza jumped out of the car and ran inside. One of the Sisters of St. Joseph of Carondelet came out with her and wheeled him inside. Monsignor Brouwers would never leave Daniel Freeman Memorial Hospital again.

Stinky Cheese and Radiation Burns

After 50-some years, Cathy Downey still chuckles today when she recalls "Uncle Tony's" European sensibilities.

"He sort of let down his guard Saturday afternoons at our house when he was staying for dinner," she says. "I remember a bright smile and a sparkle in his eyes. But I don't have a recollection of him getting down on the floor and building blocks or playing soccer or catch with me or anything like that.

"He loved stinky cheese and red wine, and the opera. I think 'La Traviata' might have been his favorite. He was an educator, and he was always wanting us to learn something. I also remember he was a machinist, a carpenter, a craftsman. He loved working on his car, and then he also built things for us at our home: a chest of drawers inside of closets and some fences. He had all types of tools that he kept at his mother's house in her garage.

"And in the evening, he'd pray Compline [the night office ending the daily Liturgy of the Hours priests are required to say]," she adds. "He would separate from the rest of us, and would walk outside with his prayer book to read. So even as a girl, I had a sense he was spiritual, a contemplative man."

On occasional visits to the rectory of her mother's brother, Downey admits she was a little in awe with all the trappings, especially the housekeeper and the crimson colors monsignors wore. After Sunday Mass her family would have breakfast with the priests at a long dark wood table that seemed to span the entire dining room. Nearby, in a room she and her younger sister were not allowed to enter, came the sound of coins being counted from the collection.

When her uncle was diagnosed with bone cancer, however, these pleasant Catholic schoolgirl scenes were soon replaced by darker ones. After experimental radiation treatments, which were in an early stage of development, the priest would stay at their Baldwin Hills home to be taken care of by his sister Catherine, who was a nurse.

"In those days, they couldn't regulate the dosage of radiation very well, and I just particularly remember the burns in the middle of his back," Downey reports. "I remember my mom changing the dressings and actually seeing the burns and just being horrified by them. But he didn't complain."

Later, when her uncle was hospitalized, there were visits to Daniel Freeman. She can still picture his two adjoining hospital rooms — one just filled with books. Books were stacked everywhere, even on the radiator because he was working on an entry for an encyclopedia. She recalls meeting a Sister Mechtilde, who wore a white nursing habit, and how much attention all the nuns gave her uncle.

"Because my father was a doctor and my mother a nurse, they were pretty straightforward with us about what was going on with him," Downey says. "But he kept thinking that he was going to walk again. He had been praying to some African martyrs, and he really believed that he was cured.

"I think my father more than my mom was being much more stoic about it," she adds. "Even at the age of 12, I was aware that it was something he really needed to believe, but that he wasn't going to recover."

She recalls her Uncle Tony's "delight" in going back to St. Paul's for his 25th silver jubilee celebration as a priest in late 1963, which was soon followed by a final relapse.

"I actually remember visiting him within 24 hours of his death at Daniel Freeman," Downey confides. "And, again, he was talking about the opera. That's probably why I remember it."

Good Patient

Back in the late 1950s and early '60s, Sister Mechtilde Gerber was a young nurse on the medical/surgical floor of the newly opened Daniel Freeman Memorial Hospital. She would visit Monsignor Brouwers when he came in for chemo and radiation therapy, and later when he was confined to the hospital. Although not assigned to his floor, she would sometimes even give him a bath when there was a nursing shortage.

"It was the beginning of the chemo era, and so they were trying different things," she reports. "Chemo was well known by people, but it was not effective then. Chemo patients used to be terribly sick to their stomachs —

not just one day, but for a couple of days. And radiation, too, was a far cry from what it is today."

These early treatments were difficult for patients to endure, but Sister Mechtilde was well aware that the sufferings and complications caused by multiple myeloma were even worse.

"Bone cancer is very painful," she explains. "It's like every bone hurts you. And the bones get very frail, so that if you move too fast you can break them. My sister, who also died of multiple myeloma, broke her two hips when a nurse was just moving her. So it's extremely painful."

She says Monsignor Brouwers was not a "big complainer" about his pain. In fact, he spoke little of it.

"People here thought he was a very good patient, yes," she recalls. "And they all liked to go and help him. He was a special patient not only because his physician, Dr. Downey, was on our staff, but because he was just a real good person. A very, very gentle man.

"The sisters on his floor loved to go in and talk to him because he was so spiritual," she says. "So when he went into a coma and died, we thought 'Thank God it went fast.'"

Late-in-Life Inspiration

Sr. Antonia met Monsignor Brouwers in the late '50s, when she was Mary Clarke Brenner, a 29-year-old Beverly Hills wife and mother. She sought out the director of the Propagation of the Faith about how the Archdiocese of Los Angeles could assist the missionary efforts of Maryknoll Sisters and Sisters of Perpetual Help in Korea. The regular reader of "Mission Chats" and the priest struck up an immediate friendship that would grow until his death.

After Monsignor Brouwers was hospitalized in November 1962, the housewife visited him every couple of days, patiently waiting outside his room if "more important" relatives and members of the clergy were talking to him. She got in the habit of coming to Daniel Freeman late at night and early in the morning, bringing along two of the priest's favorite treats: banana bread and Canadian bacon.

"In a hospital and a jail, you find out who really loves you," he would say between bites.

As their relationship deepened, so did the topics of their conversations.

"We talked about the state of the world," Sister Antonia recalls. "He talked about the missions and the good people who go to the missions. He talked like he wrote about the tragedy of a world of consumers that allowed people to die of hunger while others overeat.

"He spoke constantly of the misery that is around the world, and us not being able to see it and just go by it. At one time, people could say they didn't know. But he said no one is excused today when all you have to do is pick up a newspaper or *Life* magazine and see the faces of the starving looking at you."

During the last year of his life, Monsignor Brouwers became her spiritual advisor and social justice mentor. He talked passionately about the unfair distribution of wealth in the world, racial injustice against black Americans and Hispanics, and the Catholic Church's responsibility as the one true universal Church to curb such horrendous wrongs.

These one-on-one bedside discussions would radically alter Brenner's upper-middle-class life.

A dozen years later, after a divorce, she took the priest's name, becoming Sister Antonia, and eventually formed a non-consecrated religious order called the Servants of the Eleventh Hour. Since 1977, the outgoing former Los Angeles socialite has lived in a cell inside La Mesa State Penitentiary in Tijuana, ministering to some 6,000 killers, thieves, drug dealers and other criminals.

"Monsignor Brouwers was my inspiration," she reports. "He talked about the days of God and our role in this world. How we are all born to be holy, and we're all born to be saints. And that each one is called to give all that they have as Jesus did.

"He acknowledged that there would be oppositions and crosses and anguish and tears. But all that would be usurped, you might say, by the love of God in knowing that Christ is always with us. Because Christ is all that is worth living for. Christ is all that is worth dying for.

"That was his motto," she says. "That was his life. That's the way he lived it, and that's the way he died."

XII

Chapter Twelve
Paralysis and Death

With few medical records still available to document the progressive course of Monsignor Anthony Brouwers' multiple myeloma — especially as it reached the terminal stage — there exists considerable disagreement about when his spine actually broke and the priest became completely paralyzed from the waist down.

Monsignor Lawrence O'Leary, the former archdiocesan associate director and director of the Propagation of the Faith, believes it was not long after his coworker made his fourth visit to Africa, returning home in the fall of 1962. "He was in the hospital because he wasn't feeling well. I think they had given him all the radiation treatments they could," he says. "As I recall, it happened on the feast day of the Immaculate Conception, December 8, 1962. He sat up in bed and bingo! It broke. So he became a paraplegic.

Monsignor Brouwers is surrounded by lay missionaries he helped train.

"That was very hard on him, naturally. I had just gotten a new Ford Galaxy, so I would go down to Daniel Freeman once a week to take him out for a ride. I learned how to lift him from the wheelchair into the car. He loved watching the planes taking off and landing at the airport. That's when he told me he envied me because of all the trips I would take to Africa."

Paralysis and Death

But the Lay Mission-Helper and physical therapist who gave Monsignor Brouwers treatments the last six months of his life says her patient did not actually break his back until a few weeks before he died.

"It probably happened during the time that he was getting chemo or radiation to try to stop the cancer from moving on," Fran Laterza speculates. "And he probably had a lot of osteoporosis in the bones. So that all he did on that particular day was reach up from his bed to the [therapeutic] 'monkey bars' and he got severe pain. From then on, he was paralyzed.

"I think the bad crack happened probably after I brought him back to the hospital. Then the paralysis was really total. Before he did have some weakness and paralysis, but he was still able to walk a little. Otherwise, he wouldn't need me to help him with the active, passive and resistive exercises to both of his legs."

And Sister Antonia Brenner, who became a confidant of the bedridden priest at the end of his life, says the paralysis had more to do with surgery doctors performed after the break. "The reason he was crippled is because he was in such terrible pain when his back broke," she recalls. "And when his back broke, there was nothing the specialists could do. They couldn't even put a brace on him. So they decided to operate and cut the nerves because they thought he only had days to live."

Active Until the End

Whatever account is most accurate, Monsignor Anthony Brouwers remained fairly active until a few weeks before his death.

On November 3, 1963, the Propagation of the Faith director addressed a crowd of 10,000 children in the Los Angeles Sports Arena from his wheelchair at the first Children's Mission Celebration. He thanked and praised the parochial school boys and girls for leading the nation in donations to the missions.

The Tidings, in its November 8, 1963, issue, reported that Monsignor Brouwers spoke vigorously and earnestly of the "700 million children in the world who are hungry and, more seriously, without love or appreciation of God."

The dying priest pointed out that the world was really divided into givers and "getters."

"The greatest kind of giver is the one who gives to strangers across the seas, across the world," he declared. "You are helping strangers you'll never

At the first Children's Mission Celebration in 1963, Monsignor Brouwers spoke to 10,000 boys and girls.

see and who'll never write you notes. You can only expect to see them in glory before God in heaven.

"Then," he went on, "you will be surprised to see the people you have helped — those with no clothes, no education, the cold and the hungry for whom the world does not care. But you are reaching out to these strangers, not because you know them, but because of God, whom you do know and love."

Five weeks later, on December 8, Monsignor Brouwers celebrated his 25th silver jubilee as a priest with a Solemn High Mass in St. Paul Church. His longtime close friend Bishop Timothy Manning preached the sermon and half-a-dozen other priests acted as concelebrants and deacons. Later that evening, he was the guest of honor at a two-hour reception in the parish hall.

The Propagation director also kept up his writing. His last "Mission Chats" ran in *The Tidings* on January 3, 1964. Titled "Pope's Trip Echoes Magi's Journey," the four-column piece gave a detailed profile of the political and religious character of the divided Holy Land recently elected Pope Paul VI was about to visit.

The tone was mainly educational, probably giving readers more information on Jordan and Israel than they ever wanted to know. ("The Holy Land today constitutes two separate nations. The larger [37,000 square miles, about Indiana's size] is the Arab Hashemite Kingdom of Jordan, a constitutional monarchy of some 1,700,000 inhabitants.")

What is perhaps most remarkable for a Catholic writer of the day came towards the end of the piece. "The Crusades were a tragic attempt by Europe's Catholic monarchs to recapture the Holy Land," Monsignor Brouwers wrote. He stressed that the wrongs done to the Arab people over "darkened ages in history" will not be erased by a three-day visit from the pope.

But the Rome-educated priest ended on a typical elegant note:

"Like the Magi of old, Pope Paul today celebrates the manifestation of the Son of God by coming humbly and bearing the gifts of a new peace for Christian peoples everywhere, at the very places where long ago the King of Kings was born, lived, died and returned from the dead.

"Before heaven, and slowly before men, Pope Paul's journeying to Bethlehem, Nazareth and Jerusalem will never be forgotten, and shall surely presage a dawning of the Light of the World deeper into human hearts, and further around the world."

'Merciful' Coma

On January 3, a Friday, Monsignor Brouwers was preparing a lesson for the Lay Mission-Helpers class that evening at St. Paul's when he suddenly felt weak and experienced severe abdominal pain. He was rushed back to Daniel Freeman Memorial Hospital, where doctors confirmed an infection in his kidneys had reoccurred. The priest was quite distressed while receiving transfusions, but he also spoke as optimistically as ever about returning to the parish and his work, according to a letter Monsignor Harold Laubacher, associate director, wrote a few weeks later to Lay Mission-Helpers stationed around the world.

When X-rays were taken the next day, however, a huge cancerous tumor

Monsignor Brouwers suffered five years with bone cancer.

was discovered in his chest. The priest remained conscious and lucid much of the following week. His nurses suspected he was experiencing considerable pain, but he did not complain, probably because he wanted so badly to return to St. Paul's. But by the end of the week he worsened, and his doctors suspected cancer cells had finally reached his brain. His sufferings were described as "quite acute" on Friday and Saturday.

"That night he went into a deep merciful coma, which persisted over the weekend until the day of his passing to his reward at approximately 3:45 p.m. on January 14th," Monsignor Laubacher reported. "With him at the moment of his death were Mother Mary Rosaleen [his nurse] and Father Patrick Kelly, the chaplain at the hospital."

From left, Cardinal McIntyre, Monsignor Brouwers and Monsignor O'Leary.

Chapter Thirteen

Testimonials

Monsignor Brouwers was buried at Calvary Cemetery in January 1964.

On a Thursday morning, two days later, Monsignors Laubacher and O'Leary, the two associate directors of the Propagation of the Faith, celebrated a Solemn Mass for parishioners at St. Paul Church. The superior of the White Fathers — the missionary order Monsignor Brouwers had worked closely with for nearly two decades — preached a moving sermon comparing the Los Angeles priest to Christianity's first legendary missionary.

"The love of Christ impels us on," Father Peter L'Heureux began, quoting from "The Second Letter to the Corinthians." Then he said, "St. Paul, the great apostle, never spared himself. He worked incessantly in health and in sickness to establish the Church far and wide, to bring souls to God.

"It cost him dearly, but he had to go on. His love of God made him spend himself completely and solely, and prompted him to the greatest sacrifices. For Love of Christ impelled him on.

"Today we are gathered here to pay our final homage to the memory of a great man, a true friend, a zealous pastor, a widely known Propagation of the Faith director, a missionary completely dedicated to the works of the missions," he said. "To spread the faith throughout the world was his greatest desire, and no effort — not even life itself — was too much."

Father L'Heureux pointed out that this Angeleno had never, in fact, directly served in the mission fields himself. But his zeal was so great and his dedication so sincere that like St. Therese, the patroness of the missions who never left her cloister, he did more for the missions in his short career than many missionaries who had labored for decades in mission lands.

"If we try to find out what really was the driving force behind Monsignor Brouwers' great zeal for the missions which impressed all who knew him, I think we have it in the very words of the great apostle St. Paul, 'The love of Christ impels us on,'" he said. "He lived these words every single day and found in this love of Christ and souls — souls in the greatest need of help, those in the mission lands — the strength to sustain his untiring zeal to expend all his energies with simple, cheerful determination that no difficulty could phase."

The priest noted that the record of "this noble man of God" was truly impressive. Beginning in the early '50s, he had founded some 200 Mission Circles throughout the Archdiocese of Los Angeles — bringing to local Catholics a greater awareness of their responsibilities to the poor in undeveloped nations.

Monsignor Brouwers' "remarkable optimism" also enlivened the local Holy Childhood program in parochial schools to the extent that year after year the Los Angeles Archdiocese topped all other dioceses in the United States and world in raising money for the missions, according to Father L'Heureux. And his weekly "Mission Chats" column in *The Tidings* inspired thousands of readers to think beyond their parish boundaries and view the Catholic Church as truly universal.

"Beyond doubt his greatest, most difficult, most challenging and most rewarding undertaking is the Lay Mission-Helpers Association and Mission Doctors Association," the superior stressed. "The problems involved in bringing such a project to fruition were astounding, but with tireless unflinching zeal in the face of tremendous difficulties, he took upon himself this colossal project with self-effacing modesty. He founded this organization, recruited the first members and trained them with consummate skills, and he did so to the very end.

"Today, thanks to him, the Lay Mission-Helpers and Mission Doctors are one of the largest and most promising organizations of their kind in the world," he said. "More than 100 teachers, nurses, doctors and many other skilled and trained personnel, infused with the highest ideals, are doing excellent work in many mission lands in various parts of the world. Yes, indeed, the love of Christ and of souls impelled him on."

That afternoon St. Paul's parishioners filled the Los Angeles church again to say the Rosary for the cleric who had been in failing health since he became their pastor in 1959.

On Friday afternoon, what Monsignor Laubacher called "the most wonderful tribute of all" to his boss took place. Some 600 Sisters of St. Joseph of Carondelet, who had cared for the terminal patient at Daniel Freeman Memorial Hospital, Dominican Sisters of Mission San Jose, who had taught young Tony at Sacred Heart School, along with other nuns gathered for a recitation of the Rosary.

And that evening, priests led by Bishop Timothy Manning prayed the Office of the Dead for their departed brother.

On Saturday morning at ten o'clock, a Solemn Pontifical Mass of Requiem was offered at St. Paul Church. Cardinal James Francis McIntyre, the authoritarian churchman a 41-year-old Monsignor Brouwers had persuaded to send out lay missionaries, presided, while Bishop Manning was the celebrant. Father Henry Alker, delivered the eulogy.

Comparing his friend's life to the joyous, sorrowful and glorious mysteries of the Rosary, the priest described the founding of the Lay Mission-Helpers and Mission Doctors as a "courageous" act.

"His health began to fail, but this did not dampen his ardor or cause him to be discouraged," he said. "Nothing could stop him in the pursuit and fulfillment of his apostolic ideals. The charity of Christ pressed him on as with holy restlessness he continued even on his bed of pain, sanctified and sanctifying through his intense suffering."

Father Alker also drew a nineteen-hundred-year spiritual line from the Church's first missionary to Monsignor Brouwers.

"It was most appropriate that he be assigned as pastor to the church under the patronage of St. Paul," the eulogist noted. "Like St. Paul he was a 'vessel of election' apostle of the gentiles, preacher, writer, man of God with indomitable will, determination and dynamic drive for souls.

"How truly he could say at the closing of his life: 'As for me, I am already being poured out in sacrifice, and the time of my deliverance is at hand. I have fought the good fight, I have finished the course, I have kept the faith.'"

Testimonials

A Missionary's Grave

One of the most moving tributes to Monsignor Brouwers, however, came from *Tidings'* staffer Al Antczak, who penned the last "Mission Chats" in the paper's January 24, 1964, issue. With the understated headline "The Rain Falls Softly on Missionary's Grave," the column began by reporting that last Saturday in the rain the priest was buried at Calvary Cemetery in East Los Angeles. Bishop Manning intoned the final prayers, while priests chanted the responses.

Under a canvas shelter beside the grave, and in the open rain, stood some of those whose lives had been touched by Monsignor Brouwers: Lay Mission-Helpers, Mission Doctors, Mission Circle supporters, and Mission Men and Mission Ladies. There were also the sisters who had cared for him and taught him.

"All recited the final Our Fathers and Aves with the bishop," Antczak wrote. "The soft rain became harder. Its sound from hitting grass and canvas blended with the murmur of the prayers. Like the falling of the rain, so too was the surge of prayer in distant hearts and at foreign altars far from this graveside."

There, in fact, were telegrams from Rome, Washington and Oakland along with onionskin aerograms from Johannesburg, South Africa; Nairobi, Kenya; Tena, Ecuador; and a host of other Third World outposts. "All in Umtali" were grieved, wired Bishop Lamont. Bishop Angelo Barbisotti from Ecuador lamented, "The missionary work of the Church has lost a real friend."

In closing, Antczak pointed out that the "great theme" of Monsignor Brouwers' preaching and teaching was the unity of the Mystical Body of Christ:

"It had really started long ago in his home in Lincoln Heights in Sacred Heart parish there," he observed. "It had taken him the long years of study in seminaries here, in Washington, in Rome.

"He had walked the primitive roads and mission trails of Asia and Africa amid the poverty and loneliness of the missionaries. He had continued ever more intensely through the years in this apostolate, even until he could follow it only from a wheelchair along the frontiers of sufferings.

"The winter rain fell softly at Calvary last Saturday," the journalist concluded. "It fell on a missionary's grave."

Making a Dream a Reality

In his October 3, 1971, parish bulletin, Monsignor John Connolly, pastor of St. Jarlath Church in Oakland, wrote about a classmate of his who had died too young. The two seminarians had met at the North American College in Rome in 1935 and were ordained together on December 8, 1938. Over the next quarter century, the priests continued their friendship from opposite ends of California via letters, phone calls and occasionally visits.

Some 10 years before he died, during a visit to San Francisco, Monsignor Connolly's classmate spoke about a dream that seemed bizarre to the Oakland priest. "He told me he was thinking seriously of organizing lay missionaries for Africa, people with specific talents, such as doctors, nurses, photographers, carpenters, secretaries and the like," the pastor recalled. "He had no organization and no money. I thought he was crazy but didn't have the heart to tell him the hard truth.

"Tony made his dream a reality and me a believer in the stuff of which saints are made. A group of [sponsors] backed the venture from the start to this day. There was no lack of volunteers for the temporary missionary endeavor. A program of solid preparation weeded out the unfit and prepared the fit. In his last months, Tony pushed himself about his room, fighting crippling cancer, still guiding his dream.

"Funny, isn't it," the Oakland priest wrote, "how God takes priests like Tony home early and leaves fellows like me behind. It's for sure I feel very humble when I think of my brother priest and his crazy dream."

In a May 14, 1982, short article in *The Tidings*, Cardinal Timothy Manning pleaded that "the memory of Monsignor Brouwers must not die from among us." A close friend and confidant, the cardinal lamented that many would only recall his

Cardinal Manning called Monsignor Brouwers the "first lover of the lay mission movement."

name or the fact that he founded the Lay Mission-Helpers and Mission Doctors associations. But to others — himself included — Monsignor Brouwers would be enshrined in their hearts as none other.

In words as carefully crafted as his homilies, Cardinal Manning wrote, "He lived for the missions, offered a nobility of suffering for the missions, sidestepped any personal ambitions for the missions and died as the first lover of the lay mission movement."

Then he made a more intimate observation.

"Each [Lay Mission-Helper and Mission Doctor] was a personal brother or sister to him, and he shared their lives, their concerns, their labors. Day in and day out, the writer of this memoir shared the dreams of his heart, watched the squandering of his strength in the realization of them. He loved him dearly.

"The Archdiocese of Los Angeles, too, reaps the harvest of his priestly oblation," the cardinal pointed out. "May he remember us still."

On the 25th anniversary of his death, a final tribute to Monsignor Brouwers was published in the Los Angeles Archdiocese's weekly paper. It ran on January 13, 1989, in the editor's "El Rodeo" column with the one-word headline "Remembering."

Al Antczak, now *The Tidings'* editor, wrote that Los Angeles was becoming "New Yorkized" with its traffic gridlock and housing "greedlock." He noted how the gracious mission arch was being supplanted by the graceless steel cloud. And with a generation's passing, many memories were fading.

"In all of this, the heritage of the Church of Los Angeles should not be forgotten," he wrote. "It should not be forgotten that there were holy men here like Anthony Brouwers."

After ticking off his accomplishments as the local director of the Society for the Propagation of the Faith — including the fact that more than 600 Lay Mission-Helpers had served in the missions since 1956 — Antczak described the priest's last and most personal struggle.

"His final missionary labor was on the frontiers of suffering," wrote the editor. "He was stricken with spinal cancer and continued to work from a wheelchair. Five weeks before he died he preached at a great children's mission celebration in the Sports Arena. He died January 14, 1964. He had been a priest for 25 years and 37 days."

Antczak reported that there was only one known memorial to the man — a ward in the mission hospital in Likuni, Malawi.

Msgr. Brouwers, His Memory Lives

BY CARDINAL TIMOTHY MANNING

The memory of Monsignor Brouwers must not die from among us.

To many, only his name will survive. Others will identify him as the founder of the Lay Mission-Helpers and Mission Doctors associations. For a few of us who remain, there is a place in our hearts in which he is enshrined as none other.

He lived for the missions, offered a nobility of suffering for the missions, side-stepped any personal ambitions for the missions, and died as the first lover of the lay mission movement. Several times he journeyed to mission lands, surveyed where Lay Mission-Helpers and Mission Doctors might best be used.

GR. BROUWERS

He was inspired in the program for training them. They had a primary call to holiness of life out of which their apostolic activity would flow. Each one was a personal brother or sister to him, and he shared their lives, their concerns, their labors.

Day in and day out the writer of this memoir shared the dreams of his heart, watched the squandering of his strength in the realization of them. He loved him dearly.

The Archdiocese of Los Angeles, too, reaps the harvest of his priestly oblation. May he remember us still.

MAY 14 1982

Cardinal Manning urges *Tidings'* readers not to forget Monsignor Anthony Brouwers.

Testimonials

"Here, his memorial is that lay persons still volunteer to become Lay Mission-Helpers and Mission Doctors and go forth," he observed. "Los Angeles is changing, but it should not be forgotten that there was a holy man here named Anthony Brouwers. *Que en paz desance.*"

Chapter Fourteen

A Theology of Mission

When Father David Ayotte became the archdiocesan director of the Society for the Propagation of the Faith in July 1999, he knew "very, very little" about the man who half a century earlier had energized — and revolutionized — the local Mission Office.

He did not know that Monsignor Anthony Brouwers, realizing how vital it was to keep ordinary Catholics informed about missionary efforts worldwide, had written a weekly column in *The Tidings* from 1948 to 1964. He was not aware of the battles the priest waged with local as well as national church leaders to send lay men and women into the pre-Vatican II mission fields. And he had no idea how long his predecessor had suffered before succumbing to cancer.

In 1955, Monsignor Brouwers snaps a candid shot of an African wood-carver.

But, most of all, he did not know how many other priests, religious and ordinary Catholics who knew Monsignor Brouwers personally considered him a holy man.

"My sense from talking to all these people was they saw him as a saint," says Father Ayotte, who served as the Propagation of the Faith director here for five years. "I was hearing that this diocesan priest had a spirituality of mission that would be more common in religious communities that are missionary focused. It was just burning within him, even through his own sufferings."

Then in 2002, while doing the annual spring cleaning, Mission Office workers found a couple of boxes overflowing with Monsignor Brouwers' original notebooks and writings, aging photographs plus articles written about him and the organizations he started and strived to keep alive. At the time, the office was in a period of upheaval itself, with officials trying to decide if the Lay Mission-Helpers Association should follow the path of the Mission Doctors and separate financially from the Archdiocese of Los Angeles. (In October 2003, the Lay Mission-Helpers Association did become a 501 (c) 3 independent entity.)

"So I started reading his writings, which were very, very inspiring in the sense that he was very involved in the protection of Lay Mission-Helpers and Mission Doctors," Father Ayotte reports. "I just said, 'My gosh, the guy was very visionary for his period.' The full staff started praying, asking for his help. And it just seemed a lot of things started to come together for the Lay Mission-Helpers moving towards independence.

"We also found all these little index cards he wrote his training class notes on. A lot of them talked about suffering, the classic spirituality of the cross. There was a sense in his spirituality of the caring suffering in the missions. And he saw his own suffering as not something as a scourge, as it was a gift given to open up and provide opportunities for others. He was developing a whole theology of mission as a spirituality of mission. He saw that we can't be Christians unless we have that dimension within ourselves.

"So when we came across those boxes, there was just a sense of his presence and protection — not only in the office, but in shaping the future of the Lay Mission-Helpers and Mission Doctors," the former director adds. "There was a sense that he had a vision that was even bigger than what we're currently living."

A number of elements of that vision particularly struck the priest.

Forming Mission Circles to fund religious missionaries serving in under-developed countries was brilliant for its time, he says, as was the later development of Mission Men and Mission Ladies (known today as the Lay Mission-Helpers Guild) to sponsor individual lay missionaries. His observations as early as the late 1950s about Protestant denominations being light years ahead of Catholics in their missionary efforts also turned out to be prophetic.

Moreover, Monsignor Brouwers was before the Second Vatican Council's radical reforms giving the laity leadership roles in their parish and diocese, along with repeatedly stressing in his writings and talks the universal nature of the Church.

"He began the Lay Mission-Helpers and Mission Doctors with an experience of wanting to serve first, because that's what the bishops were asking for," Father Ayotte says. "But then his understanding of mission grew.

"And I suspect that when you come alive with mission, you get closer to a sense of who God is. Because God's encounter with creation is missionary from the beginning. Trinity is missionary in its nature. The life of the Trinity is going out of itself and pouring itself into all creation, renewing.

"The mission of God — missio Dei — is the root of all mission," he points out. "It's not our human effort. It's the moving of God using us as instruments, not manipulative but calling us to cooperate with him. It's the action of God within his loving of himself that pours himself out and renews the universe, the creation."

Father Ayotte stresses that the foundation of all mission work begins with God's own eternal mission. It is simply God being God.

"Monsignor Brouwers encountered something that wasn't only the epiphany of the Marian Congress that brought him more alive," he observes. "He met God in experience, and it just gave him, I think courage is too shallow of a word. It wasn't courage he simply experienced. He saw something and thought 'This is meaning for my life.'

"It brought him alive, and he wanted to draw everyone into it. Mission does that. Mission really converts us. When he went out to the mission fields, Monsignor Brouwers experienced his own renewal."

Missionary zeal has always been central to the renewal of the whole life of the Church, according to Father Ayotte. But many Catholics — including a number of priests, bishops and cardinals — did not see it that way in the 1950s, and still do not today.

Thinking out loud, the priest says, "It's funny," smiling. "You would think that Monsignor Brouwers' cancer and conflicts would have wiped him out. But it seemed that every affliction he had around him, whether personal or political, just made him struggle harder.

"His life shows that leadership can be one of the strongest opponents to the renewal of the Church. But if the seed is actually from God, it will continue to bear fruit. And the seeds from Monsignor Brouwers just keep bearing fruit."

Lay Mission-Helpers carry their faith to the missions in their hearts, even if they can't master the art of carrying water on their heads, as this African women has.

Chapter Fifteen

Gauging Holiness

What — or who — is a saint?

The word sanctus first shows up in the Old Testament to mean the Israelites, God's chosen people. In the New Testament, during the beginnings of Christianity, it refers to the followers of Jesus. In one of his letters to the Corinthians (2 Cor. 13:12), Paul used the term, referring to the Christian faithful.

But after Christ's death, it quickly came to describe only martyrs, those who readily died for their religious beliefs. St. Stephen, the first Christian martyr, was stoned to death after supposedly proclaiming that "God cannot be contained by human-built walls," meaning the Temple of Jerusalem.

After Constantine made Christianity the official Roman religion in the fourth century, so-called "white martyrs" could also be viewed as saints. Starting with the veneration of Martin of Tours in 397, who was said to have given away half of his cloak to a beggar, saints could die of natural causes as long as they lived exemplary lives and practiced great acts of austerity and penance. St. Anthony, the father of monasticism, was a widely recognized saint. And many hermits were worshiped for their virtuous lives.

The veneration of saints reached its zenith between the sixth and tenth

Friends believe Monsignor Brouwers lived a life of virtue.

Gauging Holiness

centuries. With no formal process for declaring a person holy, the ranks of the heavenly swelled to include bishops, scholars, missionaries and virgins. Popular opinion of who was a saint, along with a couple of undocumented miracles, could get almost anyone on the "canon," or fast-track list.

Relics were traded and sold like baseball bubble gum cards. The most common trips were pilgrimages to shrines. Every town and guild had their own patron saint. Some still exist today, such as Hadrian, the former pagan Roman military officer who was broken limb from limb by order of his commander after he was baptized. Appropriately, he was, and remains today, the patron saint of butchers.

With abuses running rampant, local bishops became more involved in the whole process, officially declaring who was and who was not worthy of sainthood. And by the turn of the first century, even the Holy Father took an interest in canonizations. In 993, Pope John XV personally canonized Ulric, bishop of Augsburg, only after demanding concrete proof of the prelate's piety. This investigation and declaration is recognized as the first formal papal canonization.

Papal canonization was the only legitimate one, decreed Pope Gregory IX in 1234. More than three centuries later, Pope Sixtus V put the Sacred Congregation of Rites in charge of processing candidates for canonization. More recently, Pope John XXIII called for a revision and simplification in the Church's 1918 Code of Canon Law, which systematized the canonization process. And in 1983, these changes finally took effect under Pope John Paul II.

Research and Miracles

But the process of canonization is still no cakewalk. In fact, author Tom Morgan, in his 1994 book *Saints: A Visual Almanac of the Virtuous, Pure, Praiseworthy and Good*, describes the supposedly simplified practice of making someone a saint a procedure that remains today "as bureaucratic as getting a bill through Congress."

It can start, simply enough, with any Catholic who believes that a certain deceased person has lived an exemplary Christian life and has exhibited a reputation for holiness (*fama sanctitatis*) or is a martyr. The petitioner contacts the local bishop, who assigns a "postulator" to oversee the investigation of the life and writings of the person: *Did the individual perservere in his or her faith until death? Did he or she live a life of heroic virture, going beyond what is expected of ordinary Christians?*

If there is clear evidence this is the case, the whole stage moves from the diocesan to the apostolic level in Rome, after the petitioner agrees to bear both moral and financial responsibilities. The latter is no small matter, since the postulator must move to Rome to continue his sacred duties, and future investigations may — and often do — drag on for years.

Once in the Eternal City, the postulator collaborates with the Congregation for the Causes of Saints, made up of cardinals and bishops, to produce a *"Positio,"* a biography of the life and virtue of the person. This lengthy printed exposition, which is the formal argument for sainthood, is presented to the Congregation and the body's historical and theological consultants for evaluation and judgment.

If the candidate receives a "degree of heroic virtue" verdict — signifying that the Church, through research, historical study and theological reflection, recognizes extraordinary moral goodness in the person — he or she receives the title "venerable servant of God."

This accolade may sound impressive, however, it is just the first hurdle in a three-stage process. The pope alone decides who gets to be beatified and canonized. And for all non-martyr candidates, the proof that the "finger of God" *(digitus Dei)* approves can only come from miracles — one for beatification, two for canonization.

Miracles show that through the intercession of the candidate God has indeed performed an extraordinary act. Once again, there are investigations, first at the diocesan level by a physician who evaluates medical evidence, eyewitness reports and other documentation. If there is no scientific explanation for the cure — or other seemingly supernatural happening — then the case returns to the Congregation for the Causes of Saints in Rome for a second round of rigorous theological and medical scrutiny. After the entire Congregation decides that a true miracle has occurred, its positive judgment is passed on to the Holy Father, who declares the candidate "blessed."

According to the *New Catholic Encyclopedia,* "When the pope declares someone 'blessed,' conferring that title on a venerable servant of God, he declares that for the pastoral good of the Church this person is worthy of emulation and can enjoy a public cult of praise within the confines of a particular diocese, region or religious family."

To move from beatification to canonization requires a second alleged miracle, which is investigated as thoroughly as the first. If the pope issues a bull of canonization, he declares that the blessed is a saint worthy of venera-tion by the whole church. Canonization, which is the goal of all "causes," is the Church's undeniable statement that the new saint stands before the throne of God in heaven.

The actual canonization usually takes place in St. Peter's Basilica with a Pontifical Mass. Although marked with great solemnity, it is basically a simple ceremony. A short biography of the individual is read. The litany of the saints is sung. And the pope makes a solemn pronouncement of saint-hood, with the congregation responding "Amen."

Chapter Sixteen

Heroic Sanctity

Monsignor Brouwers
and Cardinal
Manning were
steadfast friends.

Archivist Monsignor Francis J. Weber has spent his entire priestly life researching, studying and writing about the history of the Catholic Church in California along with its major and minor players. And he is convinced that holy men and women of faith really do share a heroic, larger-than-life quality.

"One of the qualities that the Vatican looks for in the life of a saint is the practice of heroic virtue," he explains. "Heroic virtue is the practice of ordinary virtue in a special way. In other words, if the average person is charitable, saints have to be super charitable. Because 'heroic' means over and above the ordinary."

Monsignor Weber points out that Rome does not require that an individual be heroic in all virtues. Most saints, in fact, were known for embodying only one or two in a special way.

"I would suspect Tony Brouwers' virtue would be evangelization and helping others — the ordinary things we associate with the missionary," he says. "And those he certainly did heroically. He was a visionary, sending the laity into the missions. Great people have vision, and nothing gets in their way. Mother Teresa was the same way. They're visionaries who don't get slowed down because of opposition — and he had a lot of opposition.

"He was a pioneer, a man who wouldn't say 'no' when it came to the Lay Mission-Helpers and Mission Doctors. No question about it, it was unique, and it demonstrated that he understood missionary work for what it was. He always felt there was more to the missions in undeveloped parts of the world than preaching. You can't preach the Gospel to hungry people. You can't preach the Gospel to sick people."

The archivist believes that Monsignor Brouwers was not only ahead of Rome in sending lay volunteers to impoverished lands, he was also a step in front of John F. Kennedy and his high-profile Peace Corps.

"It was a heroic thing to do in the pre-Vatican II Church," Monsignor Weber stresses. "But he saw that lay men and women could be a different kind of witness and even more effective sometimes than religious missionaries. He understood the notion of 'go preach the Gospel' was not limited to priests, brothers and sisters."

Bishop John Ward agrees that his boyhood buddy from Lincoln Heights practiced extraordinary virtue as a priest in the Archdiocese of Los Angeles for 25 years — especially in regards to the creation of the Lay Mission-Helpers and Mission Doctors. The forces he faced were formidable. "It would have been easy for Tony just to say, 'Forget it,'" he points out. "But he fought through it."

The retired bishop says the last time he saw the priest alive illustrates how much of a fighter he actually was, even at the end with his body racked with cancer, his senses numbed by pain medications:

"I went into his room at Daniel Freeman, but he was in and out of it. And all of a sudden, he woke up when I was there: 'Oh, Jack, how are you?'

"I said, 'Fine, Tony. I'm on my way to a confirmation.'

"'That's good, Jack.'

"'I don't want to disturb you.'

"And he said, 'No, no, Jack.' Then he said, 'Go back to the chancery office and put up with those sons of bitches! Just offer it up.'

"And I thought, boy, here's a guy who's a real saint. Those were the last words that he spoke to me. He died the next day."

Bishop Ward was also awed by the way Monsignor Brouwers accepted his years of suffering with equanimity. He never complained or even talked about it, although the bishop knew that every movement must have hurt him. The most he ever heard the terminal patient say about his cancer was "Ah, it's there, but what can I do?"

Bishop Ward goes so far as to call Tony Brouwers a perfect priest.

"He was constantly concerned about people and their spiritual development," he reports. "But his spiritual direction was down to earth. He didn't take up any of the theologians of the day. No, just the fundamentals of what the Church wants. And if there was any obstacle, for example, if people got themselves into an invalid marriage, he would do everything he could to get them out of it.

"Everything that was priestly was first in his life. I mean, his Masses, confessions, attending to the needs of his parish as well as all his mission efforts. He was not off on big vacations for himself. No, he was at work. He just gave a heroic effort at whatever he did.

"Other priests thought so highly of him, they'd come to the chancery to have him hear their confession, which tells you a lot," adds Bishop Ward. "Tony is still on my mind frequently. Very frequently. I think about what a perfect priest he was, who used every ounce of God's grace for his priesthood in service of the people. And I think that someday we'll be praying to him as a saint."

Total Acceptance

Monsignor John Sheridan was also taken by his friend's sufferings.

"I never saw anyone more resigned than Tony was," he says. "He was a young man struck down with cancer. I saw him toward the end, and we were talking. He knew the potential he had, but he was totally accepting. And, strangely enough, he never complained. Never."

"I remember distinctly this one occasion when we did talk about it. He said, 'Well, John, I'm so grateful to God that I've had all these opportunities. So I just ask his help along the way.' Oh, he absolutely knew it was terminal, but it wasn't like he lacked hope. His outlook was just total acceptance."

The pastor emeritus of Our Lady of Malibu parish believes his fellow pastor must have simply decided to work up to the very end, which took a certain fearlessness and fortitude.

"I think he was a man who definitely found and formed and nurtured that continuum between his thinking, his prayer life and his ministry," he says. "One can see an individual's sanctity, and there's no question about Tony and his great compassion for people."

Monsignor Sheridan — whose own weekly column, "The Question Box," ran for many years in *The Tidings*, and who authored a number of

Monsignor Brouwers shares an audience with Pope Pius XII.

Pope John XXIII bends an ear to listen to the Los Angeles priest.

scholarly yet popular theological books — believes that Monsignor Brouwers' writings were equal to his lectures and sermons. In his "Mission Chats" columns, the director of the Propagation of the Faith was able to communicate in a down-to-earth conversational way the Christian — but human — side of missionaries.

"He got across that the Church is the community — the whole community of the faithful in which the bishops and priests play an important part as divine facilitators," he points out. "But they're nothing else, only servants of God. So this man got us in touch with that reality at a very pedestrian, foot soldier level. And he did it at a time, before Vatican II, when the hierarchy was wrongly believed to be the essence of the Church.

"So if there's anyone who should have a biography in this archdiocese, it would be Tony Brouwers," he says, grinning and shaking his head. "It's too bad that there aren't more of us around who remember him."

Sister Antonia Brenner goes so far as to call Monsignor Anthony Brouwers the "initiator" of the lay movement in the United States. Even though he was a conservative Catholic and a conservative priest, he believed in the laity. He was not afraid of the laity. In the eyes of the foundress of the Sisters of the Eleventh Hour, that makes him not only brave but holy.

"He was anointed by God," she says. "He had a great gift that touched everyone. It touched me: his loyalty to the Church, his loyalty to friendship, spending himself out for the sake of others and making decisions that went against the structure of the Church.

"His great love of the poor endeared me tremendously to him. While he would criticize the rich, the poor he never criticized. For Monsignor there was only one question: *Am I my brother's keeper?* Are you responsible for the world's misery, or are you going to do something about it? It's the question that God himself gave to every human being to answer."

The former Beverly Hills housewife has answered the query by living in a Tijuana state penitentiary for more than a quarter-century, ministering to inmates and guards. When asked why, she says it goes back to her friend and spiritual mentor Monsignor Anthony Brouwers. He spoke to her being — her very soul — which is why she took his name. Because like no individual before, he believed in the good she could do with her life.

Sister Antonia believes her namesake is a modern-day martyr.

"He served right to the very end of his life," she says. "His body was tired. He was irritated at not being able to walk. He was frustrated by others who didn't have his vision for the laity and the missions. He was anguished. But he went over the top of whatever kind of depressive feelings that would be natural for him to have.

"Because all that mattered to him, he told me quite clearly before he died, was doing the will of God. Not for tomorrow; not for a week from now. But for this very moment and the moment after that and the moment after that. Until those moments tick away until months and years and his whole life goes by.

"So he was truly a martyr, always seeking to do the will of God," she stresses. "He was poured out like an offering on the altar."

A True Missioner

For Monsignor August Moretti — the self-described "punk" in the chancery when Monsignor Brouwers was director of the Society for the Propagation of the Faith — there is no doubt that the priest was a virtuous individual.

"He was very unselfish, even though there might have been some suspicion among clerics that he was doing all this for *Tony's* glory, that was the farthest from the truth," says the pastor of Assumption of the Blessed Virgin Mary Church in Pasadena. He was really about serving the Lord. Because he understood better than many of us the need to share the faith with people — not only through a check or a charity, but through human beings."

Monsignor Moretti says the priest was much more than the administrator of the local Mission Office. He was a missionary himself because his entire priesthood was centered on spreading the word of Jesus Christ — not only through religious missionaries but also through the example of the laity.

"It's almost like St. Therese of Lisieux used to say," the seasoned pastor observes. "You don't have to be in the mission land to be a missionary. And I think Tony was offering his suffering and his indescribable pain caused by the spinal cancer for the work of the missions. It was a very great challenge for him to do that. But that's what saints are made of — people giving themselves to God. And Tony gave himself to God.

"I saw him only twice in the hospital," he adds. "He was very serene. And I know he was at peace with himself and the Lord."

Monsignor Lawrence Donnelly, who lived with Monsignor Brouwers at St. Agnes rectory, can never forget when the director of the Society for the Propagation of the Faith asked him to take over his demanding post. It was the early summer of 1959, and cancer was beginning to take its toll on the priest's stamina during his African, Asian and South American trips to visit Lay Mission-Helpers and Mission Doctors.

Monsignor Brouwers walked into his office in the Marriage Tribunal, sat down in a chair and said all the travel was getting to be too much. Then he said he would love to have the younger priest become the Propagation's next director.

"Tony, I would ruin what you've done," Monsignor Donnelly responded. "I don't have your organization. I couldn't be flying around like you are because my father is dying. I wouldn't have the zeal, just by nature, meeting different people all over the world. You've done so much great work here. There's no place in the United States where the Propagation of the Faith Office is like here. I would just ruin what you have done."

When his friend tried to object, Monsignor Donnelly mouthed something he had been thinking about for a long time.

"You know, I lived with you Tony, and I know that you're a holy man," he said. When his old rectory mate chuckled, he went on: "I mean that with all my heart. You are a saint, and I just can't succeed the work of a saint. I'm not worthy of it."

After Monsignor Brouwers blushed a bit, a grin came over his face and he changed the subject.

"He took it very graciously," Monsignor Donnelly recalls today. "He wasn't any different to me after. I think he understood, especially with my father's situation. But he was a sweet, gentle man, and I know that hurt him. Tony was just an apostle with an intense love for the Church. He would do anything to spread the faith. That's why I say he was a saint. He *was* a saint."

Mike O'Callaghan, a diocesan priest from 1948 to 1970 and a canon lawyer, also refers to his friend Tony Brouwers as a "saintly man." The founder of O'Callaghan Travel Service and college professor remembers him as even tempered with a great deal of patience. He cannot recall a single outburst of anger or anything that even indicated his friend was upset about something.

"My memory of Tony is of the highest regard," he says. "Always a nice smile. Bright and lively. Full of information to talk about. His conversation was always uplifting — something about the missions or the Vatican Council. He indicated always a very, very logical mentality."

But most of all, O'Callaghan was impressed by his holiness.

"Tony Brouwers was the kind of person and priest that I would have no hesitation endorsing his cause for canonization," he says. "Why? Because of the way he behaved: his actions, his perseverance, his good will. He loved the missions. He loved to bring people to Christ and to bring Christ to them.

"And he did unusual things. The Lay Mission-Helpers, Mission Doctors, Mission Circles and Mission Men and Women. One man started all that. My God, how many lay people have gone to missions because of him?"

After a while, O'Callaghan observes, "He was a visionary — one hundred percent! He reached way beyond the boundaries of the Archdiocese of Los Angeles. He reached out to the world way beyond what any priest that I know ever did."

Disciples and Witnesses

"What Monsignor Brouwers did is he gave you the courage to be a disciple — not a disciple in terms of going out and thumping a Bible, but a disciple in terms of going out and witnessing through your own profession."

So says Herb Sorenson, M.D., one of the early Mission Doctors, who volunteered in Africa.

"What he was doing in our classes was 'discipling' us," says the OB-GYN specialist. "He was telling us there is more to life than just going to work and doing your daily job. There's a spiritual dimension to life that most people miss, which he wanted to give to us. And here was an opportunity to go over to another continent and country and to serve — to serve as an example, because we would be watched tremendously.

"He gave us a view of what we used to call the Church comfortable and the world comfortable, the Church uncomfortable and the world uncomfortable," he explains. "And he was preparing us to function in the uncomfortable part of the world."

The reason Monsignor Brouwers was so convincing about all this was because of the example of his own steadfast spirituality, according to Dr. Sorenson. He was able to take the heart of what it meant to be a servant of Jesus Christ and bring it down to where "the rubber meets the road."

"I think his legacy was to follow the words of Jesus to go forth and make disciples," the retired San Diego physician reports. "Plus, he had the vision to trust the laity. It's like the quotation on the Lay Mission-Helpers ring, which I still wear, from Corinthians: 'For we are God's helpers.'

"God could have organized all of these missionary efforts. He could have done all these things. But he ordained that we were to do the work.

And Monsignor Brouwers trusted the lay person to do it."

The priest trusted Lillian Casey. He sent the Douglas Aircraft production worker to be a Christian witness to the poor of Kenya and Ghana. And she would continue to serve in Israel and Appalachia after his death, until she had logged two decades as a Lay Mission-Helper.

Asked shortly before her death in February 2004 why she spent 20 years of her life as a lay missionary, an incredulous expression came over the 89-year-old woman's lined face.

"Because he was a saint!" Casey shouted. "That's why. He showed us that everyone is God's child."

Appendix: 'Mission Chats'

For 15 years, Monsignor Anthony Brouwers — as the local director
of the Society for the Propagation of the Faith and founder of the Lay
Mission-Helpers and Mission Doctors associations — penned his signature
"Mission Chats" for *The Tidings*. That adds up to more than 700 weekly
columns which appeared in the Los Angeles Archdiocese's newspaper.
Topics ranged from the Mau-Mau uprising in Kenya to the deadly Piranhas
that inhabit Amazon rivers, from the relentless persecution of missionaries
in Red China to the challenge Muslim nations pose to the Catholic Church.
His first "Mission Chats" ran September 24, 1948; his last January 3, 1964.

One Priest –
1,500,000 Hungry Souls

By Msgr. A. J. Brouwers
Director, Propagation of Faith

It is our privilege daily to read laments sent by missionaries all over the world.

These are by no means mere "begging letters." They are but the fraternal sighs of a fellow priest caught up in the woes and poverty of his suffering flock. Living intimately the beggar's life of his people, he feels with a priestly heart the hunger, nakedness, sickness and misery. After some years of this, the good missionary with a soul overwhelmed with what he sees and lives all around him sits down to unburden himself with a letter to America. Hope alone in some instances will carry a man on!

Only this morning a letter arrived from Bishop Cialeo of Mutan, Pakistan. The jovial, zealous Bishop, in recent months in this country to beg a mite for his millions of starving Moslems and now returned to his diocese, writes, "My American experience makes me see even worse than before the conditions of these poor people. What a difference in life! Many have less than the minimum necessary for existence. How they live is a wonder, but their life is certainly most miserable."

What most Indians earn in a year is thoughtlessly spent by an American couple for a dinner and movie on a Saturday evening.

One to 1,500,000

We think the following letter from a discouraged priest in East India is far more eloquent than any words of ours. It comes from Father Pagano working these 15 years among some of the poorest of the poor along the Godavary and Kistna Rivers of India.

"The big problem, which unfortunately seems to interest only God and myself, is to know how to go about evangelizing all alone an immense parish of 1,500,000 souls spread over a radius of about 60 miles. These people belong to every caste and every religion. There are almost 70,000 Protestants of various sects with hospitals, churches and schools, but as yet I have only 2,000 Catholics and two small elementary schools.

"Forty-two miles from my residence on the Godavary River there is an island where last year I baptized 200 pagans. On the island 700,000 pagans live, and there could be a wonderful conversion movement among them if only I could send them a priest. A man of God provided with essential needs could make 10,000 converts there in five years. The Lutherans, the Salvation Army and the Baptists go around in autos equipped with loudspeakers; they show religious films, open leprosaria, set up TB hospitals, and everywhere are constructing fine churches.

Dream and Reality

"Bhimavaram, where I reside, can count only 300 Catholics among its 50,000 inhabitants. The Mass I say for my Christians has to be at an altar set up in the main room of my house. I had a large hut which served as chapel, but the last cyclone spread it over the ground and I have not the funds to reconstruct it.

"My house is just opposite the train station which handles 1,000 passengers daily. For five years I have dreamed of building a neat little church facing this busy spot, with small cupola and bell-tower; I am sure the pagans would enter out of curiosity. The educated Hindus here have great respect for the Catholic Church, which they have come to know in other parts of India. Many times they have asked me when I am going to start making use of the mission grounds for a hospital, orphanage and church. More and more I am convinced that the sight of Catholic activities in full bloom would draw many to the Church.

"But the reality is another thing. I am alone in the midst of this immense harvest, alone with my worn-out bicycle, the unintended discarded gift of a confrere two years ago. When it refuses to carry me, I drag it along beside me in my visits to the 25 villages I must care for.

Do You Believe?

"My Catholics on the island in the Godavary River have sent a petition to Rome to have a priest assigned to them. As yet I am alone in the midst of this abundant harvest. If no one comes to help, the hour of Providence may pass and there will be nothing to do but grieve over lost opportunities. Pardon me for sharing such personal thoughts and pray for me, please."

Do you believe deeply enough in the Communion of Saints and the Mystical Body to pray for Father Pagano?

That a few dollars from you would cheer him up immeasurably, goes without saying.

How the Evil Mau-Mau Works in Kenya

By Msgr. A. J. Brouwers
Director, Propagation of Faith

In recent weeks the public has heard of the Mau-Mau secret society in Kenya Colony.

Kenya Colony is a pleasant land under British control, on the Indian Ocean in East Africa. Its population is 4,000,000, sparsely scattered through its broad plains and rolling hills and up its mountain slopes.

Already over 340,000 of Kenya's Negroes have become Catholics, and prospects for the future are bright.

But now comes the news of an enemy at work, sowing his usual cockle. The Mau-Mau originated in 1947, but until a few months ago it was a negligible factor in Kenya native society.

Presently these fanatics, fired by undefined hatred for all white men, fanned by weird superstitions and ancient native witchcraft, have broken into public view. Arson, pillage, and murder are the fruits whereby they are recognized.

Members Terrorized

It will be helpful, as we hear more of their criminal antics, to know something of their nature and purpose.

Mau-Mau initiates must take an oath, with all the fearsome ritual of old African paganism. Until recently only trusted volunteers were admitted to this secret society. Now however, even teenagers are forced into membership, under threat of torture and death. Once a member, he is terrorized by the fear of consequences.

The Catholics who have fallen victim to their force and their atavistic fears, are not easily persuaded to renounce the society. The reason is that the oath taken by the members includes a solemn resolve to apostatize.

Until recent months the Mau-Mau of Nairobi (capital of Kenya) followed chiefly a political agitation calculated to expel all white men.

Now it has penetrated the Vicariate of Nyeri and carries on a death struggle with Christianity under pretext that this religion is a white man's belief and non-African.

They Must Deny

Catholic members are required to throw away their rosaries, medals, crucifixes, and all objects of devotion, the possession of which is to the African a profession of Faith. They must deny Christ and place all their obedience and trust in the Mau-Mau leader, Jomo Kenyatta, a seditious man of no religion nor morals.

Bands of Mau-Mau have invaded a Catholic school and burned sacred objects and have attempted desecration of a tabernacle.

Always alert, the missionaries have organized "Days of Return" for the unwary apostates who have been taken in by the immoral leaders. Days of public penance and general Communion are followed to supply spiritual force against the Mau-Mau insanities.

Bishop McCarthy, C.S.Sp., of Zanzibar, has issued a formal letter condemning the society and placing the sanction of excommunication upon Catholic initiates. This was done because of the society's anti-Christian attitude and conduct.

There is no denying the anti-religious and blasphemous nature of the Mau-Mau.

'By All Means'

Like the watchful shepherds of the flock, down the corridors of the Church's suffering ages, Bishop McCarthy said to his people:

"It is not necessary, my brethren, to tell you that the prosperity of peoples, tribes and nations comes from God and from His blessings. If a people does not attribute its prosperity to Him, but rises up against Him, its prosperity is but a semblance, certain to disappear as soon as it shall please the Lord to confound the proud insolence of His enemies.

"Being mindful of your baptismal vows, by virtue of which you are children of God and heirs to His Kingdom, and also of the Sacrament of Confirmation, when you were enrolled as soldiers of Christ, we appeal to all Christians, particularly those living in Nairobi, to be faithful and true to your solemn obligations and to resist by all means in your power the evils of the 'Mau-Mau' association."

The Only Way

This new evil of Kenya seems but a weird clamor from out of Africa's long ages of superstition. But the white man has left upon sensitive native memories a black record of cruelty, injustice, and bloodshed.

Still the missionaries and their Church must not suffer for the crimes of a few Europeans of the past.

Kenya's current anxiety over the Mau-Mau deserves a rosary or two, don't you think?

"Such as these are cast out only by prayer and fasting."

'Civilization's Cradle' Almost Non-Catholic

By Msgr. A. J. Brouwers
Director, Propagation of Faith

Most of the ancient history of the human race was enacted around the Mediterranean Sea.

Today, living leagues distant from the lands near the cradle of civilization and remembering so little of high school history, we are hardly conscious of the races and countries of Africa's north shore and the taciturn Near East.

Picture a large **L,** as reversed with its **horizontal** bar facing to the left instead of the right. Place the **horizontal** bar of this reversed **L** over North Africa, and the **vertical** bar over those countries directly north of Egypt.

Along the horizontal bar you would find **French and Spanish Morocco, Algeria, Tunisia and Libya.** Along the vertical bar you would read the names of **Egypt, Israel, Lebanon, Syria and Turkey.** These are the two divisions of lands we will here briefly discuss.

Those of the first division (of the horizontal bar) have a Catholic population of 1,500,000 (European generally), forming but a small minority of 23 million Islamic Arabs.

The countries along the vertical bar, chiefly Egypt and Turkey, embrace a population of 47 million Moslems, with less than one million Catholics; almost entirely of Oriental Rites.

However, more than a million Orthodox and dissident Copts also live in this area. These Christians, so distinct religiously from their Moslem neighbors, are nevertheless of the same race and creed.

In the division of North Africa, extending for 2,500 miles from west to east, are the vast French territories. Here there is a shortage of Priests, and few vocations.

For instance, **French Morocco** with nine million people has but 400,000 Catholics. Of all the countries here discussed, it has the greatest number of Priests. Over 300 of them, mostly Franciscans, are almost evenly divided into those engaged in parochial work, and with teaching and works of charity.

Spanish Morocco has but 66 Priests to care for its 100,000 Catholics among 1,200,000 Moslems.

Algeria can claim only a 10% Catholic minority in a population of eight million. There are 650 Priests, half of whom are engaged in parish work.

Few Vocations

Tunisia can claim but 7% of its 3,250,000 population as Catholic, chiefly of south European stock. Vocations are alarmingly few, and its 300 Priests in parish work are insufficient.

Libya is a recent sovereign State, completely Moslem except for 400,000 Catholics of Italian origin. The Franciscans work hard to keep the Faith alive and thriving.

The second area, once called the **Levant,** comprises **Egypt,** whose twenty millions is but 15% Christian. Of this percentage, only 200,000 are Catholic. The rest (2,800,000) are dissident Copts. Annually some 2,000 of these Copts return to the Church of Rome. Catholic influence is felt mostly in schools conducted by the

Religious, and in the Egyptian newspapers owned and operated in many instances by Lebanese Catholics.

The other vast country is **Turkey,** where the Catholic Church has a feeble and precarious existence. There are but 22,000 Catholics among twenty million Moslems.

Lebanon is the only land of all those here mentioned where the Christians retain a slight majority (53%). Of this percentage one-third is Orthodox. All the rest are Moslems. The government spends great efforts to keep the Lebanese in civic peace.

Syria recognizes the Catholic Church as one of the three "heavenly" religions, co-equal in theory to Mohammedanism. But there are but 114,000 Catholics among the 3,300,000 population. There is an alarming daily control of the Christian schools in Syria.

Israel is the synthetic state carved in recent years out of an Arab land. Although officially tolerant, this land where our Saviour lived and died must admit much violent prejudice against "foreign schools." There are but 25,000 Catholics out of a population of 1,565,000 Jews.

These facts and figures we have recorded, so that you will appreciate what has happened to an area of the world where before the seventh century there were over 700 Catholic dioceses and Bishops. Today of 71 millions, there are but 2 1/2 million Catholics and a few score of Bishops.

Man Bites Dog – Fish Eats People

By Msgr. A. J. Brouwers
Director, Propagation of Faith

For no special reason we are writing about fish.

If you have never heard of one vicious little devil inhabiting the Amazon jungle rivers, you have a surprise coming.

This amazing creature is called the **Piranha,** more dreaded by the natives than the most poisonous snakes or the slithering crocodile.

The piranha will attack anything large or small, living or dead. Carelessly drag a hand beside your canoe in an Amazon jungle river, and in two or three seconds a school of these little monsters will have left only a skeleton below your arm.

Finny Fanatics

The piranha measures but a foot in length, with a face suggesting a bad dream, staring eyes and a jaw full of razor-like teeth. Just the smell of blood in the water is enough in a matter of seconds to turn a calm pool or smooth river into a whirlpool of ferocious piranhas. One snap of its ugly jaw, and a whole finger is gone or a chunk of flesh the size of an egg.

Stories are told of the dreaded piranhas that send shivers along one's spine. They are known to have stripped all the flesh from a drowned man, without removing the clothing. Such stories are countless, and none of them could possibly have been exaggerated.

They will bite off a dog's tail, or tear to pieces larger fish caught on a hook. They devour one another, thus making it impossible to contain them in aquariums. Their sharp teeth will cut in two with one stroke the fisherman's hook.

Out of the water, they make throaty sounds, and savagely attack anything within reach. One writer reports that he saw a severed piranha head continue to snap for over a minute.

Jungle Missioners

Piranhas are but one of many dangers that lurk under foot and overhead in the "green hell" that is the vast Amazon jungles and river-ways.

In several areas even today, there are head-hunting natives, completely naked creatures who delight in the raw flesh of animals and man. In recent decades their number has greatly decreased, but we are told that no cautious white man will venture into some jungles for fear of the unseen natives more than of the lurking reptiles and smaller life.

Still, in many Catholic souls there throbs the zeal of Christ, and despite the history of murder, martyrdom and extreme sufferings in the past, valiant priests, brothers and sisters this very moment are braving every danger to teach and uplift such jungle wildmen.

How many millions there are, far from the big cities and inhabited areas of Brazil and Peru, who shall say? But, there are millions we know, still ignorant of Jesus Christ and His Church, as if they lived not in the mid-20th Century but still in the centuries before Columbus and Pizarro came upon them.

They Need Help

The missionaries are men and women from Latin America itself, from Europe and the United States, representing many societies and religious communities. In their difficult, dangerous and oft discouraging efforts to teach savages the simplest truths of religion, they need the ardent prayers of the universal Church.

January is traditionally dedicated to the Holy Childhood of Jesus Christ. As an afterglow from the love and piety that were yours during the recent holidays, please remember in Jesus' Name the Missionaries and their plight.

They number 100,000 men and women, gone from homes and native lands all over the world. Whether in civilized or barbarous lands, they need vitally our prayers, our sacrifices and constant generous alms.

By the scores of thousands, they have for love of immortal souls, surrendered home, nationality, native tongue, friends, civilized and accustomed conveniences, and many another earthly boon, not for a few years of overseas service, but for life.

The least we can do for them, laboring somewhere and everywhere in our stead, is to help them spiritually and materially.

This is the program of the Society for the Propagation of the Faith, the Holy Father's own Mission-Aid organization.

Storm Clouds Gather Over Promising Japan

By Msgr. A. J. Brouwers
Director, Propagation of Faith

In these first days of August some ninety million Japanese are remembering an anniversary.

They are remembering but not celebrating!

For, you see, ten years ago on the feast of Our Lady's Assumption in 1945, Japan was shattered with grief and defeat. On this day the Emperor stood before a microphone to tell a crushed people that the peace of the vanquished had fallen upon them.

A few days before Nagasaki and Hiroshima were blasted with America's A-bomb. At 11 a.m. on August 9, 1945, Nagasaki was absorbed in the buzz and hum of midday city life. Two minutes later (11:02 a.m.) the atmosphere was violently blasted with atomic fire and explosion.

In a few seconds Nagasaki, Japan's foremost Catholic community, lay twisted, blackened and splintered. By nightfall 70,000 Japanese had met their God. Of this number 9,000 were Catholic, 7 per cent of the nation's total number.

History's first atomic bomb had fallen almost directly over the sanctuary of the Urakami Catholic Church in Nagasaki.

New Conquest Begun

With the end of the war, the Church surveyed her losses to find over a million square feet of churches, schools, hospitals, convents and other institutions had been demolished.

Twenty thousand Catholics had been killed, and there were only 500 priests to care for a hundred thousand scattered over numerous islands.

Then, something extraordinary happened. Missionaries, accustomed to indifference from the non-Catholic Japanese, were being swamped with requests to study Catholic doctrine. Whole villages were instructed and baptized.

Answering urgent requests from Japan's Bishops, as many priests as possible were sent to reap the ready harvest.

Today, in a short decade since defeat in 1945, the Church counts 200,000 Catholics. Each year in the last five, over 10,000 catechumens have been baptized.

Diocesan priests are adding to their numbers, as are the forty-two societies of men missionaries. Sisterhoods are also multiplying. In fact the proportion of Japanese Sisters is three times higher than in the United States. Here is a breakdown of personnel:

> Clergy 1,144 (262 Japanese)
> Brothers 388 (228 Japanese)
> Sisters 3,449 (2,464 Japanese)

There is a total of 1,500 in the seminaries and religious novitiates.

Japan is blessed with unusually apostolic lay apostle groups. The Legion of Mary exists in about half of the parishes. The JOCIST movement has 83 active sections. A national organization of Catholic Students is doing what it can, to counteract Red influence in schools.

Catechists are being specially trained at Nagoya. They attract and prepare prospective converts and help distribute 300,000 leaflets each month to non-Catholics.

Catholic institutes of charity have more than doubled since A-Day. Education on every level has marvelously grown, with 11 colleges and two universities.

Storm Clouds Gather

Yet, despite this rapid growth in numbers, students of the Japanese scene see low clouds of terrifying storm gathering over the islands.

Recently a Communist leader boasted to a Catholic priest in Japan that the Reds would take over this intelligent and energetic nation in three years.

Japan suffers, as no other people, from devastating post-war ills. Millions are unemployed. Hunger stalks the land; over-production of peacetime articles flowing from converted wartime industries has Japan bulging with hardware and merchandise.

Japan needs foreign markets for her industries. Twenty per cent of all her food must be imported, for lack of land to cultivate. Her diet is insufficient and of the poorest quality.

Japan's population continues to grow by over a million per year, despite an annual 1 1/2 million abortions and the wide-spread practice of contraception.

If and when the economic and social pressures can no longer be contained, a terrifying upheaval will take place.

Observers of Japan fear that Communism, growing stronger with each day, will dominate the entire nation. This would mean the loss of the whole of Asia to the Catholic Church for centuries to come.

Situation Urgent

Japan must have more land on which to support its hardworking millions. Emigration would help, but the more favored nations have slammed their doors shut to the idea.

Her condition is grave and urgent; it is feared that another war might well be in the making in these critical years.

What a tragedy, perhaps written at Yalta, if Japan's growing Catholic Church should be suppressed and destroyed by Asiatic Communism!

If so, Japan will suffer a defeat more terrible and lasting than that sadly recalled in this August of 1955.

You See Holiness In the Missions

By Msgr. A. J. Brouwers
Director, Propagation of Faith

Nothing so argues the Church's divine character as the holiness of so many of her members.

As in Europe long used to the fruits of Christ's truth, the mission lands too may boast of their saints and holy people in recent ages.

India has her first and as yet only canonized saint. He is St. Gonzalo Garcia, a Franciscan Brother martyred over three and a half centuries ago.

Gonzalo was born in Bombay State in 1564. He was educated by the Portuguese Jesuits at Bassein and at 16 he joined their mission band to Japan as a lay catechist.

For eight years in Japan he was held in high esteem by the humble and the royal.

Later he became a merchant, and soon amassed a fortune. But Gonzalo hungered for the apostolate.

Surrendering his wealth, he joined the Franciscans as a Lay Brother, and once more was off to Japan.

When in 1596 the Japanese began their bloody extermination of all Christians, Gonzalo was among the doomed captives.

On February 5, 1597, he, with 22 others, was crucified, holding in his hands a rosary blessed by Pope Adrian VI. For 40 days the martyrs' bodies hung on their jibbets, without signs of corruption. The Japanese martyrs were canonized by Pius IX in 1862.

Teenagers Martyred in Africa

African's first saints were the Martyrs of Uganda. One of them was their staunch catechist Charles Lwanga.

With him 12 page boys of the court of King Mwanga were burned alive near Kampala City in British East Africa, on Ascension Thursday, 1886.

Because these teenagers refused the pagan King's sinful designs on them and would not deny their allegiance of God's Church, they won the martyr's crown. Today these Blessed are the glory of a proud people, and the promise of the total conversion of Uganda.

IN OUR OWN DAY, reports tell of numerous others in China, Vietnam, Oceania, Korea and elsewhere, all of them noble souls showing forth the mark of holiness of God's Church.

For example, there is the Indian Poor Clare Sister Alphonsa, who died only in 1946. In 1930 on entering the convent in South India, she did so "to become a saint . . . otherwise, why should I become a nun!" Her short convent life was consumed with sickness and suffering, which she bore with saintly patience and cheerfulness. Rome has authorized the formal investigation of her fame for sanctity and reported "miracles." Pilgrims from all over India and Pakistan crowd her humble grave.

Dr. Atiman Is of Africa's Best

In the same spirit of heroic living and marked holiness, there lives today a remarkable man in Karema of Tanganyika. He is Doctor Adrian Atiman, who last year received one of Britain's highest honors for distinguished service to his fellowmen.

As a boy Adrian was captured by Moslem slavers and carried northward across the Sahara. There he was ransomed by the White Fathers, baptized and educated.

After winning his medical degree, at the expense of the Missionaries, Doctor Adrian was sent to Central Africa.

He was shocked with what he saw in Zanzibar.

Only 70 years ago, one could still see along the roads corpses of black slaves, who had died of inhuman treatment from their Arab buyers.

Since then Dr. Adrian has labored with skill, great success, enduring love and unfailing sacrifice in the area of Karema. He is today at 90 the greatest, most beloved layman of Catholic Africa.

Read a missionary's tribute to him:

"The folks of Karema confide to him all their secrets and troubles. He is the father of all. With his own money he supports many poor families. He uses his influence as peacemaker in family squabbles . . . He works all day and even at night. He never refuses. For Adrian the eighth-hour day does not exist. I believe our Adrian is the most sympathetic person in the whole of Africa."

Of such is the Mission Church. Her good and holy people are an encouraging sign of our times. They are a pledge of a bright future.

In this New Year do your share spiritually and materially to make Christ's Great Dream come — the holiness and sanctity of mankind.

You Have to Smell Poverty to Believe It

By Msgr. A. J. Brouwers
Director, Propagation of Faith

Liturgically, these are days for charitable and generous thinking. Charity and generosity are of the very essence of Christ's law of the gospel.

There is no escaping the final judgment at the end of time, when Christ shall face each of us, to ask as He promises: What have you done to your fellowmen, these who are My little brothers?

If the accounting of our life's behavior suffices, heaven shall be ours; if not, everlasting hell.

It is a frightening ordeal to envisage. The use for our neighbors of talents, time, energies, purses and material possessions shall be the measure of eternal reward or damnation. The reason is, says Our Lord, that doing and giving to fellowmen is doing and giving to Himself.

In view of this fearful eventuality, one is not a little alarmed to observe the selfishness, indifference and thoughtlessness of men towards fellowmen.

To examine just ourselves, privileged and blessed members of Christ's Body, the Church, we wonder even more why so few are touched by the poverty and miseries of the masses on earth. We are simply without human explanation for the hard hearts, the selfish persons and tightly-zippered purses of so many.

You Can Smell Want

Why is it so hard to recognize poverty when it is so common? Why so difficult to see one's duty to alleviate as best we can?

Why, at the approach of the beggar (or the special collection basket), a certain mechanism in us flies into action: immediately we measure and weigh, argue pro and con, to decide how small a coin we can lavish upon an evident want or misery?

Not so at all, when a luxury for self is contemplated. Only crumbs pushed indifferently from tables of plenty go to the Jobs of this world.

Reputable reporters tell us of the poverty and miseries here or there, but we take it with a generous grain of salt.

Some of us walk through the filth and shambles of suffering and hasten from it lest we be properly disturbed. A few know the odors and embarrassing touch of want and refuse to admit its existence.

No one denies that many are the generous souls who know and respond to poverty at our elbows and across the seas. We speak here of the half, or more, who never or seldom cast a second glance at our earthly equals whose miseries cry to heaven for mercy or vengeance.

How few really understand the sweat, the inhuman working conditions, the lives shortened by drowning or sharks, by explosions or mine cave-ins, to provide milady with her string of pearls, or the master with raw rubber for his white-wall tires and shower cap?

Do we know the sacrifices forced upon starving millions to give you and me the copper for kettles, telephones and TV sets, the dyes for clothing, the sponges for the bathtub, the gold for our watches and jewelry, and the diamonds for the bride's finger?

Some Don't Care

Who measures the cost in human blood to make life comfortable and soft for the few millions who can purchase so painlessly the products made from the raw materials so expensively pulled from the earth?

Who can know until it is observed at close range the real price of such objects, so easily procured and so lightly treasured?

Do we honestly grasp the meaning of want? Do we feel with and for the untold millions whose life of drudgery, misfortune and need is no more their doing or choice than is ours of freedom, prosperity and plenty?

Many do not know the needs of the world's poverty; some do not care. Others know but refuse to lift a finger or open a tight purse.

The present writer, on journeys through the mission lands, has had the privilege of rubbing shoulders with the reality of poverty. To see it in all its stark realism is not enough; one must smell and touch it before the mind drinks in the realities of the senses.

I have watched crippled, diseased and leprous adults and children in long lines stretched across compounds into the thick tropical forests, waiting dully half the day for a clean bandage, a few pills or an injection.

I have marveled at the black giants bathed in perspiration, while digging and drilling a rich gold vein, a mile into the earth's belly.

I wondered too who might be the more foolish, the diggers in the fetid holes, or the Americans who shipped every golden bar at $38 per ounce to Fort Knox, there to be put back into the ground.

Poverty Everywhere

Photos tell little of the reality of the world's poverty, for filth in color is not repulsive, nor does one see the emptiness of a suffering face, nor smell the foul odors inseparable from poverty.

You must sicken a little at the raw flesh of yaws on an African's thigh to appreciate the mercy of a soothing bandage and salve.

You must hear the grunting coolie burdened by 150 pounds on his back, and watch the emaciated Arab like a senseless ox turning all day in the sun a waterwheel on the Nile.

You must step into the native hut, smaller than an American kitchen, where 15 Indians live their entire lives.

See, too, the pulling, dragging, burdened men, women and children everywhere, and you begin to know the meaning of poverty and injustice.

See it all, even as the aloof tourist, and you understand a little better the appeal of Communism, with all its false pretenses and hopeless promises.

As never before, the Church of Jesus Christ must reach out with the quick hand of the Good Samaritan, to all the millions of suffering sons of God.

Last year over 80 millions were aided in the mission lands by our missionary priests and religious.

We trust that one serious Lenten resolve will be to beg from Jesus on His Cross something of the divine commiseration that was His. With this grace you will love the missions more and give more selflessly of yourself and your means.

The Master Plan of God Makes Us All Missioners

By Msgr. A. J. Brouwers
Director, Propagation of Faith

Much of the secret of Communism's victory over one-third of mankind is due to its Master Plan.

Recent feasts of Pentecost and Trinity Sunday remind us of the primary role of God's Church. Is the entire Church, we wonder, equally convinced that Jesus Christ, the Son of God, founded and became "incarnate" in His Church and her members in order to win the world spiritually to Himself?

Such is the Master Plan of God. Nothing less can be understood from Christ's command to the Apostles as He stood poised to ascend to the side of His Father. "Go, teach all nations . . . baptize them. . . . All power is given Me. . . . I give it to you to accomplish this plan. . . . I shall be at your side to direct and accomplish this plan."

SUCH IS the plain meaning of Jesus Christ, if we may be permitted a paraphrasing.

This apostolic spirit, this unique and essential purpose of the Church of God, is an undeniable and inescapable objective for every member of the Mystical Body of Christ, which is the Church.

Pope, bishop, pastor and parishioner share it equally, although the priesthood possesses special powers and prerogatives of jurisdiction. The Sacraments of vocation to convert the world, however, are Baptism and Confirmation, not Holy Orders.

THE MASTER PLAN of the Catholic Church is the missionary purpose planted in all Catholics everywhere and always. Pope Pius XII stated clearly in 1956: "The missionary spirit and the Catholic spirit are one and the same thing. . . . Catholicity is an essential note of the true Church. This is so to such an extent that a Catholic is not truly faithful and devoted to the Church if he is not equally attached and devoted to her universality, desiring that she take root and flourish in all parts of the earth."

The Catholic family must be missionary, in this sense. The Catholic school and parish and community too must be missionary.

The family which does not imbibe the spirit of multiplying and sweetly spreading the perfume of its own spirituality rising from its belief and prayerful zeal, fails its missionary role. The school and parish which does not teach and practice this note of the missionary, fails God and no less the un-Christian masses awaiting knowingly or not the coming of the Lord.

ONE WRITER well describes God's Master Plan as the "crescendo of assimilation of the finite many into the infinite one." The mission of the Church — to capture all the human race into the Master's net — is the vocation of every Catholic.

We think that the very salvation of the Church's members depends in large measure upon the recognition and exercise of this missionary role.

Did not Our Lord say that if we failed to profess Him before men, He would not admit knowing us or defending us before His Father in heaven?

IT FOLLOWS that the pastor, the parent and the teacher must transmit this essential spirit of zeal for saving souls to their subjects, else they fail God, the Church and themselves spiritually and perhaps eternally.

There is little likelihood that informed and serious Catholics, priests or people, will deny this missionary Master Plan of God.

The danger for all of us, however, is that we make too little of it. For example, the parent may instill only a desire to save one's own soul, and not be concerned with others. . . . it is hard enough to get to heaven oneself . . . let them take care of themselves . . . it's the job of the priests and religious. . . .

OR, TEACHERS may teach and prepare pupils over the years, and fit them for a successful and easy material life; and never inspire them with a concern and desire to advance the missionary purpose of the Church.

Often, such sacrifice and dedication are not expected and seldom mentioned in our schools.

PARISHES TOO must by sermon and sacramental life amplify the Catholic missionary spirit, in a hundred ways and on many occasions.

It is not a matter of "talking up the Missions." The Master Plan of God must permeate the members of the Church like water does the parched sands.

The **missionary** Catholic works, studies, creates, prays, worships and dreams in order that souls be saved, and Church shall grow in holiness and numbers.

AS CATHOLICS we apologize to no secular power, to no rivaling religious sect and to no disagreeing fellow Catholics for this conviction.

It is the divine command planted so deeply yet plain to see, in the whole of the Body of Christ which the Church is, that we cannot deny, minimize nor apologize out of human respect.

Do you admit and believe this divine Plan in your daily life? Do you employ your talents, profession, job, time and person to accomplish it?

IT IS WORTH considering, we assure you.

Protestant Missionaries Outnumber, Outwork Us

By Msgr. A. J. Brouwers
Director, Propagation of Faith

Many Catholics, I daresay, labor under the illusion that our foreign missionaries far outnumber and outwork their Protestant counterparts.

The zeal, organization, generosity and dedication of Protestant foreign missionaries are forever a source of amazement and sometimes envy to many a Catholic.

Lest we of God's own Church rest with imaginary laurels, we

ought to realize that we are outnumbered by at least a hundred thousand Protestant missionaries, "ordained" or otherwise, in those countries dubbed the "mission lands."

The Mission Research Library in New York numbers some 42,000 Protestant missionaries laboring in countries other than their homelands.

To this impressive number must be added at least 200,000 native Protestant ministers and co-workers in all of Asia, Africa, North and Latin America, Oceania and elsewhere.

Traveling through Africa and Asia, one quickly becomes conscious of our American Protestant missionaries at airports, along remote roads far into the bush, at well-equipped modern hospitals, schools and in compounds and mission stations that show off American cleanliness and ample evidence of a healthy flow of American dollars for their support.

Outnumbered 6 to 1

There is no doubt that as compared to some 140,000 Catholic priests, Brothers and Sisters in all of the mission lands of the world, they are in a majority.

From the United States alone, our Protestant fellow citizens outnumber us more than six times.

In the medical field for example, we count but nine Catholic doctors in the mission lands as missionaries, as compared to 500 Protestant medical missionaries, both single and with their families.

Regarding the financial support of the "foreign missions," Catholics are so severely outstripped that comparisons are agonizing.

Protestant sources recently reported that a general estimate of income for foreign missions in 1959 totaled some $220,000,000. Of this, nearly $170 million dollars came from the USA and Canada.

In the same year from the entire world of Catholics (500 millions) came some $20 million dollars. Compare the 220 to the 20 — for the entire world!

It is no consolation that 70 per cent of this world revenue for the conversion of the world by Catholics came from Americans.

Zeal Outmatched

It has been said that protagonists for the mission cause, as so many others, misuse such figures to beguile and wheedle an extra dollar from the unsuspecting.

We believe the figures evince too great a variance to suffer misuse in this instance.

One critic wrote that we Catholics are satisfied to fight Communism and less violent and more Christian opponents of God's Church with a 50 percent zeal and generosity, while the opponents demonstrate a zest and effort that approaches the 100 percent mark.

One wonders if they are not more convinced of their errors than we are of our truths!

Should any Catholic think for a moment that our divinely mandated missionary cause is oversubscribed by personnel or monetary aid, the above comparison serves to disillusion him.

To say that we have churches, schools, seminaries, institutions and the like to build "at home," is no argument nor excuse. Our Protestant friends do the same, relatively speaking.

And no one shall say that they, by and large, have more of this world's goods.

Communism has demonstrated an extraordinary sense of world mission. Indeed, the dedication and sacrifices of its zealots are nothing short of the messianic.

At Least Pray

The historical victims of the Protestant Revolt, moreover, have for centuries dis-played a zeal and readiness to give much or all for their beliefs and opinions.

We admire and commend this generosity of self on the part of the Protestant missionaries everywhere. We do not belittle at all the tens of thousands of heroic and selfless Catholic clergy, religious and laity in all the mission lands.

But we cannot but feel a sense of shame that the true cause of Divine Truth and the rare miracle that is the Catholic Church should even for a moment suffer by comparison with the giving of persons and purses by our Protestant fellow Christians.

And we would hope ardently that when God at last reveals His recording of the spiritual gifts from mankind, Catholics shall not be again outstripped.

May it never be that we of the Mystical Body shall raise less prayer to God for the conversion of the world than all Protestant bodies together.

If we cannot give self or means, we can pray. And if we pray, we (or others through us) shall learn to give self and means!

Eradication of Malaria Will Speed Gospel Word

By Msgr. A. J. Brouwers
Director, Propagation of Faith

"Cherchez la femme." We could freely translate this belabored bit of French with, "Watch out for the female."

Whatever the wisdom of the caution in human behavior, in the critical field of malaria eradication, the warning is fundamental.

In recent years under the aegis of the World Health Organization, a world-wide campaign is afoot to stamp out, once and for all time, mankind's scourge of malaria.

At first glance, you may wonder why a column committed to matters missionary, presumes to discuss a disease. I need but remind you of the legions of Catholic clergy and Religious whose precious careers for Christ have been snuffed out, severely abbreviated or rendered only partially effective because of malarial infection.

One-third Suffer

Then too, the missionary's zeal and labors are only fractionally fruitful because his native peoples are perennially or periodically so weak of body and dull of mind through malarial fever that they cannot absorb or stomach the supernatural concepts of the better life proposed to them.

Malaria is an ancient disease, said to have destroyed Alexander the Great and dismembered the Roman Empire.

Centuries ago wise heads identified it with the fetid marshes or the foulness of the air.

"Malaria" means bad air! The Greeks before Christ's time more properly identified it as a swamp disease. The French today call it *"paludisme."*

Historically malaria has not enjoyed the reputation of the spectacular. Unlike the plague, smallpox or TB, it has been a notorious but unheralded killer of untold millions.

At present 1,200,000,000 persons on earth, more than one-third of mankind, suffer or die annually from malaria.

Its victims evince no sores or wounds to move others to pity. In the dark and quiet of the tropical night, one small silent insect — the Anopheles mosquito — pierces a human skin.

Malaria parasites in the salivary glands of the mosquito are transmitted to the blood stream of the human victim. He or she now has malaria.

The parasites first develop in the infected person's liver and quickly develop and multiply in human red blood cells.

There follows a crucifying fever, diarrhea, storms of heat and icy chills, wild dreaming, anemia and, too often, death.

Millions succumb all over Asia, Africa, Latin America and Oceania each year to the onslaught of malaria infection. "Mrs. Mosquito Anopheles" is the carrier responsible for infecting over a billion men, women and children annually.

Campaign Launched

WHO has long argued that to chase this murderous pest from our globe, the nations, through enlightened organization and a universal application of insecticides, have but to break the chain of infection.

Kill the mosquito before the malaria parasite has had time to develop within its organism and become a danger for the next person bitten.

The campaign already promises to become the greatest scientific and humanitarian project ever conceived and executed by the human race.

Dr. C. A. Alvarado is director of WHO's Malaria Eradication Division. He has under him today 423 malaria experts working in 70 countries. He writes in World Health's recent special issue on malaria:

"We are engaged in a monster program. It calls for tens of thousands of teams, and millions of tons of supplies and equipment. Hundreds of millions of homes must be visited."

Moreover, to reach every hut for spraying of DDT and to do blood analysis, traversing mountains, rivers, swamps, jungles and most difficult of all through and over human fatalism, ignorance and indifference, thousands of vehicles, donkeys, camels, elephants and boats are needed.

Thousands of laboratories and tens of thousands of laboratory technicians and aides, translators of strange languages and dialects, compilers of data and statistics also are required.

Malaria eradication means also innumerable maps, charts and census files, to keep eternal vigilance over nomadic movements of people, giving lectures, holding open-air discussions with villagers and remote tribes, giving directives and generally regimenting the natively disorganized and frequently unconcerned victims of earth's worst and numerically most fatal of diseases.

Swiss Paul Muller's discovery of DDT after the last World War completely altered the attitude of modern science and medicine toward malaria. DDT made malaria control into a simple operation of spraying this residual insecticide onto the inside walls of dwellings where mosquitoes rest after feeding on human blood.

DDT's poison kills the insect, thus checking the infection. Meanwhile malaria sufferers must receive treatment to minimize the number of infected blood streams from which the insect can draw more parasites.

Meaning for Church

There are untold problems for scientists, medical doctors, the entomologists, biochemists and geneticists, as well as social workers and whole armies of local helpers and aides who must be trained to observe victims, render harmless billions upon billions of insects, organize and regiment half-willing people to cooperate in eradicating the most prevalent of the world's scourges.

All this in God's benevolent providence will aid and advance His spiritual kingdom, for the Gospel is always and everywhere more readily received where hunger, thirst and disease are not tearing human bodies to pieces.

A sound faith flourishes usually in a sound and healthy society and people. This is the meaning of malaria eradication for the objective of the Church of God and deserves therefore our attention and our spiritual support.

Acknowledgements

I want to thank Monsignor Francis J. Weber, archivist of the Archdiocese of Los Angeles, and adjunct archivist Kevin Feeney for all their help in digging out dusty files and faded photos — plus taking the time to carefully copy original manuscripts, articles and other documents regarding Monsignor Anthony Brouwers, the Lay Mission-Helpers Association and the Mission Doctors Association.

Mike Nelson and Father Anthony T. Scannell, editor and publisher of *The Tidings*, let me spend weeks going through the Catholic paper's bound volumes and clip files researching this biography. They also generously allowed me to make copies of hundreds of pages of stories at no cost. Vicky Gomez, receptionist and secretary, was invaluable in keeping the copy machine stocked with oversized paper and toner as well as the copier in good spirits.

Hermine Lees copy edited and proofed both the first draft and galleys. The editor of the Los Angeles Archdiocese's directory also put me on the right path to many critical leads and sources. Moreover, the veteran Catholic journalist was always there to share a glass of Chablis or two whenever the work was not going well.

John and Karen Chacon, steadfast friends and partners at Catholic Creative Services, also read the manuscript, offering invaluable insights about organization, style and language. Danny Lee assisted in layout and production. Eniko Gahan keyed in all ten "Mission Chats" columns listed in the appendix with nary a typo.

Last, I would like to especially thank Janice England, Lay Mission-Helpers executive director, and Elise Frederick, executive director of the Mission Doctors Association, for giving this wordsmith the assignment of a lifetime — to affirm, celebrate and bear witness to a good and, perhaps, holy man.

– RWD

Interviews

From August 2003 to April 2004, 60 interviews were conducted with the following 47 individuals, who unsparingly shared their memories of Monsignor Brouwers and other related matters. Most were in-person, in-depth talks that were taped and later transcribed.

Francesca Alioto
Father David John Ayotte
Sister Mary Helen Bauer, OP
Norm Breault
Sister Antonia Brenner
Lillian Casey
Addie Coronado
Jean Davis
Pat Devaney
Monsignor Lawrence Donnelly
Cathy Downey
Janice England
Gerry Fallon
Genevieve Ferreira
Elise Frederick
Sister Mechtilde Gerber, CSJ
Sister Maria Elena Gutierrez, OP
Ruth Kleimer
Frances Laterza
Sister Carroll Laubacher, CSJ
Paul Leehan
Hermine Lees
Mrs. Richard Lesco

John and Rosemary McGhee
Monsignor August Moretti
Monsignor Richard Murray
Mike O'Callaghan
Monsignor Lawrence O'Leary
Father Colm O'Ryan
Monsignor Francis Osborne
Bill and Jean Pawek
Don Riley
Betty Risley
Sister Regina Clare Salazar, CSJ
Monsignor John Sheridan
Sister St. George Skurla, CSJ
Herbert J. Sorensen, MD
Sister Patricia Supple, CSJ
Sister Pauleen Therese, CSJ
Chuck Walsh
Bishop John Ward
Monsignor Francis J. Weber
Don Wick
Sister Karen Wilhelmy, CSJ
Frank Zins

About the Author

Bob Dellinger has been an editor and reporter at Catholic newspapers in Los Angeles, Syracuse and Omaha. He was also a research writer at the Boys Town Center for the Study of Youth Development. On the secular side, he's been an assistant editor of *Human Behavior*, a national newsmagazine of the social sciences, as well as an associate editor of the *Los Angeles Free Press*, an alternative weekly. The Saratoga Springs, New York, native has written for the *Los Angeles Times Sunday Magazine*, *Los Angeles Magazine* and the *Los Angeles Reader*. He is currently the editorial director of Catholic Creative Services in Burbank, California. The Catholic Press Association has awarded the photojournalist first place honors in feature writing, personality profiles and cover photography.

Lay Mission-Helpers
For We Are God's Helpers
I Cor. 3:9

The oldest lay missionary ministry needs your help. Cardinal Manning called Monsignor Anthony Brouwers the "first lover of the lay mission movement" in the U.S. Catholic Church. Continue our founder's legacy of lay discipleship by supporting the nation's oldest lay missionary ministry — the Lay Mission-Helpers Association.

Please accept my gift of: ❏ $50 ❏ $100 ❏ $250 ❏ $500 ❏ $1,500
❏ other $ _____

Please send me: ❏ Information on volunteering to be a Lay Mission-Helper.
❏ The LMH newsletter.

Name _____

Address _____

City _____ State _____ Zip_____

Phone _____ E-mail _____

Make checks payable to: Lay Mission-Helpers Association;
3435 Wilshire Blvd., Suite 1035; Los Angeles, CA 90010. Contributions can be made by credit card on our website at: www.laymissionhelpers.org.
Thank you for your gift.

To order additional copies of *'For We Are God's Helpers,'* contact the LMH office at (213) 368-1870 or info@laymissionhelpers.org